A PHILOSOPHY OF THE FUTURE

Azimuth defines direction by generating an arc between a fixed point and a variable, between the determined truths of the past and the unknown data of the future.

A PHILOSOPHY
OF THE FUTURE

ERNST BLOCH

Translated by John Cumming

An *Azimuth* Book
HERDER AND HERDER

1970
HERDER AND HERDER NEW YORK
232 Madison Avenue, New York 10016

Original edition: *Tübinger Einleitung in die Philosophie,* volume I.
© 1963 by Suhrkamp Verlag, Frankfurt am Main.

CONTENTS

PREFATORY NOTE

It is always better to take your reader straight to the point and spare him a long preamble. This is particularly advisable when the book itself is offered as an introduction. If it takes a long time to get to the matter, the mind tends to refuse what is really needful.

This work consists largely of material first delivered as lectures. If the spoken word can still be heard (where it should be heard), well and good. It helps if you tell someone the way as well as point it out; yet what the voice spends only the letter preserves: *vita brevis, ars longa*.

There are many schools of thought and primers for the ascent to the heights. The steps are as old as (if not older than) Parnassus. And there are many Introductions to Philosophy that advertise themselves as such. This one is different: its prolegomena are more direct than indirect; it doesn't represent all the branches, or accord space to all the topics. Still, there's compensation, even if the approach seems rather precipitate for the first affair with wisdom. Too many guides offer roads that end up nowhere in particular; and too often the lack of any philosophy to introduce is the reason for writing an introduction to it. The kind of neutral commentary produced for the unsophisticated tends also to intimidate the reader, and the disinterested report of an impersonal and ideologically reticent narrator can obscure the matter itself.

Of course a process of instruction does emerge in the better primers of philosophy; for example, in Külpe's charmingly old-fashioned manual. There, philosophical questions are methodically categorized and the various "attempted solutions" or "movements" are assessed and pigeon-holed. Hardly adequate as education, however. It doesn't do to treat your students as unthinking children: as if there were no philosophy for adults and the only possible reader could be a raw recruit. Surely a visit to the workshop is much more helpful, and the production-line itself the best visual aid; and a voyage in the training-ship more effective than the on-shore lecture. New Year's Eve and New Year's Day, *post festum* and *status nascendi,* go best together when learning is in question. Introduction can fittingly serve as epilogue, and epilogue as introduction; at once as free and as concentrated as possible.

At times this book may prove demanding, but it will not produce slick, inclusive judgments or make the tyro a universal pundit. Instead, one of its chief features is the provision of a pattern of thought—which in no way implies the restriction and sparse diet characteristic of a positivist approach. Far from it. We are concerned here with a kind of thinking and exploration that goes to the very point rather than give up before it's in sight; that leads anew precisely to metaphysics. Not to the static metaphysics of the past, but to a much more insatiable and open form, describable only as a process which is still undecided and whose bearings are themselves still at the point of rough calculation and experiment—that is, in the introductory stage. Hence this short and more or less introductory offering. Somewhat lacking perhaps in exact indications of where we're going; possibly something of an invitation to have your cake and not eat it; intricate by design, and that throughout. Already enough for an introduction, if not for the exercise itself. *Homo semper tiro:* man is always a beginner; the world is a venture; and man's part is to give it light.

A PHILOSOPHY OF THE FUTURE

ACCESS

1. Emergence

I am. But without possessing myself. So we first come to be.

The *am* of *I am* is within. And everything within is wrapped in its own darkness. It must emerge to see itself; to see what it is, and what lies about it. It must grow out of itself if it is to see anything at all: itself among selves like itself, by which (no more in itself) *I am* becomes *we are*. Outside that being in itself dawns the world round about us, in which there are men, and below, beside or above them, things. At first they are alien: more or less repel, more or less attract. They are in no way obvious; their acquaintance must be made if they are to be known. The process by which they are known is entirely external; only thus does learning bring experience; only thus, by virtue of what lies without, does the inner self come to know itself.

This perpetual travel outwards is the way proper to man: assigned him above all that he may come back to himself and find there the profundity that is not in him only to be in itself, undisclosed. The mere *am* of *I am,* only to achieve self-awareness, must take to itself a something from without. Figuratively, too, man that is born within his own skin is born naked, and needs alien things from without: requires that with which he may cover himself, precisely in order to take warmth from his own presence and, indeed, to assert it.

No single image has arisen purely from within that would allow us to describe and express adequately that innermost speechless being-in-itself.

Such words and phrases as "narrow," "deep," "warm," "dark," "bright," "oblivion," "full awakening," "the inner way itself," are all taken from without and only then shed light on what lies within. Therefore everything within becomes conscious of itself only by virtue of what lies without. Does this not to abrogate but to make manifest its being itself. Otherwise it would remain isolate; without that being-with-us that is not "he," not "one," but "we"; without that round about us which came (and comes) to be the potting soil in which the human plant grows, and the raw material of man's house. Only then is that which environs us thought from within, so that it may come ever closer, become ever more relevant, ever less alien to man. We are all on our way to this goal; and as we set out, so we ourselves emerge.

2. Need is the Mother of Thought

That which lives is not yet alive to itself. Least of all in its own functioning. Is not aware by what and in what it has its beginning; is still in the lower depths; yet in every moment that is a moment now, is there, throbbing. This very *now* in its prompting is dark: our very *am* of *I am,* and the *is* of all that is. And that which is within, dark and void, stirs.

To be perceived is only that it hungers and is in need. Thus it moves; thus, in the darkness of the moment now lived, of the immediate *in itself* of all. And all is still built round about this nothingness; round about, though, a nothingness it does not sustain. Within there is a void that would be filled. So it all begins. So too that which is wholly within, and that which lies beneath it, in which all is wholly in itself, first unrolls above itself all that it perceives. In this way we are able to apprehend not (as yet)

2

ourselves in our own "what," but an external "somewhat," spread out in a visible field so that we meet it not directly but at least at a distance from our own darkness, and therefore without.

Then, living in mere immediacy, we stand beneath the glass from which we drink; and do so because, drinking, we are still immediate to ourselves and not so clearly visible as the glass we hold out. Hence we ourselves are still wholly below, and far less perceptible and comprehensible than everything we see before, around or above us. This very nothingness of having can cling only to what lies outside, hungering for what is without. It cannot help satisfying its hunger with what is placed without: that is, cannot forbear seizing upon things.

So, for the first time, want is appeased. All other drives are derived from hunger; and henceforth every longing turns upon the desire to find satisfaction in the what and somewhat that accord with it and are outside it. This means that all that lives must tend towards something, or must move and be on its way towards something; and that in its restlessness the void satisfies beyond itself the need that comes from itself. This kind of want is soon answered, as if there had been no question, no problem. But satisfaction is always transitory; need makes itself felt again, and must be considered in advance, above all to ensure its disappearance not merely as hunger and deficiency, but as a lack of what is most necessary.

As they worked towards this end and ceased to be mere food-gatherers (or, at best, hunters), men became for the first time creative and therefore (in this sense) intelligent. Born naked, no longer directed by instinct, in an environment of risks where every track must be observed and even the pine branch was food for thought. Their use of fire was followed by the conscious making of tools in order to turn raw materials (which seldom serve well thus) into clothes, home, cooked food, and ever new assets to be held against bare want.

Reflective labor first took the human race to a superior position historically, and allowed it to seek and to find what was wanted: need was the mother of thought.

But human thought certainly does not begin and end here.

3

It can reach beyond mere short-term cash profit. The seeker takes his time to find out what *is,* even if that which is cannot (at least not immediately) be consumed.

A case appropriately considered, appropriately solved, must first be approached; but the approach, however necessary, is not the end of the case. For even meditative thought itself, engaged though undismayed, begins with thought born of want. Then, much more singularly aroused, and indeed imagining something much more singular, thought becomes an inquiry into that in which it does not know where to turn. So wonder begins; and today still our better part is wondering. In other words: once awakened by want, thought becomes profound. Nevertheless it is true and will be in time to come that thought was born of need. We do not dance before meat—a maxim that thought never forgets. So that it may know how to return to the thing that is needful, and not soar too high. Like that of the beasts, mankind's hunger is seldom one-storied; the more men eat, the more they hunger.

3. *Seek and You Shall Wonder*

A more searching investigation, taking us along with it, is under way. It is wonder and amazement, not merely at something, but at the that and the specific what of so much of the somewhat, and in its very midst.

It happens to children—usually only for a short time, of course; later on it's not so frequent, but when it does occur it's all the more instructive and worthwhile. Not so much in a difficult as in a strange environment that is not necessarily inconsistent with us—for often the reverse is true. Precisely quite simple, even insignificant and transitory impressions can provoke the amazement in question, and start the cracks and crevices in ordinary, conventional perception. This kind of fissure usually spreads from minor, fleeting impressions, when what they seem to affirm inquiringly and to inquire affirmatively is

4

itself quite initial, though located wholly where the self-interrogator himself is.

Recurrent and ubiquitous, diffused almost at will, incomplete, this astonishment does not decay. It is entwined with the urge of wanting, but prompts with a more durable if shorter thorn. Though it appears relaxed, assuaged, wonder is ever restless, its first questioning ever constant.

Wonder favors a plain and unassuming form in which its characteristic quality—its mystery—is best disclosed. Quite without affectation, children will ask the familiar question: "Why is there something and not nothing?" And immediately mere figurative simplicity dissolves—for consider a moment: would not this possible nothing be less questionable, more reasonable? There is also the more substantial form of amazement that most of us can trace back to childhood (or at least to later childhood), and which coincides with the consciousness of being oneself—an "I." How strange it is always to have this *I* tagging along with one—how very like constantly shaking one's head in mixed surprise and dismay. A blessing perhaps, but in the guise of restraint: hardly self-evident, at any rate. Or, just as fresh, in no way erudite or abstract, there are those children's questions about *time:* time which, as they say, devours all things, and so what the child has noticed—an old car tire perhaps. Problem enough, this rusty wheel, but now it points to time—time which destroys the wheel. And what is time? Wondering, solving and yet not solving the problem, the child answers: "Time is a clock without numerals."

But the first true manifestation of authentic wonder is to be found in the contemplation of the ordinary itself, which is the earliest and, as it were, most authentic substance of this intellectual shock. In his story *Pan,* the Norwegian novelist Knut Hamsun relates a conversation between a man and a girl in a lonely country setting; it contains many such moments. The damselfly and the single blade of grass, for instance: "Perhaps it quivers slightly and makes me think—that's something: this blade of grass here is quivering." And there is the pine tree:

[handwritten margin note:] wonder at the ordinary

5

"Perhaps it has a branch that also forces me to think." And then, as the first drops of rain fall, the girl says: "Yes, just think, it's raining"—and then she's on her way. Nothing very much has happened to her, yet she has approached the germ of all questioning: the importance of not underestimating the plain and unassuming thing with its still, small voice.

In a not so very different context, Hofmannsthal noted this finely textured, all-pervading astonishment, yet found all the usual expressions (even the most sublime) too inadequate to convey its delicacy. At least that is the sense of a letter written by the poet's imaginary Lord Chandos to Francis Bacon—a letter which gradually abandons speech and consequently dumbfounds its recipient. Equivalents of Hamsun's pine branch in its prompting of a moment's thought do not merely make one wary of snap judgments and familiar, universal concepts such as "soul," "spirit," or "body." Someone who is alert, sensitized or (most important) responsive in this way can hardly endure such terms. He is one who would still be dumb, so to speak, if others had not discovered language; had not made themselves largely responsible for transforming into a pine branch that which makes man speechless; making it now (according to Hofmannsthal's Chandos) not something merely known as "a pine branch," but something that in this literary drapery has lost its individual appearance and the impact of its true word. Accordingly wonder is arrested; and in the hasty conformity of this spoken departure from wonder, the things of wonder are shut out from men, and men from them.

It is significant too that Chandos' inner surprise is mainly kindled by small things—the seemingly commonplace, the easily replaceable. "A watering can, a harrow abandoned in the field, a dog in the sun, a humble churchyard, a cripple, a laborer's cottage"—all this (too much sometimes, less would have been more than enough) evokes certain wonder in Chandos more than what would usually be recognized as exceptional phenomena. The interchangeable content of all these "impressions" shows how vague and indeterminate the effect of the matter in question is; it is still the same in itself. And wonder at all these things has nothing (or nothing as yet) to add to the source of sudden amazement itself, apart from the faithfully recorded impact of the objective state of having been amazed. Later, of course, this state is filled out with questions that are far from vague, having a causal structure and empirical application.

If the intellectual shock of first amazement, together with whatever provoked it, does not last, the unremitting uniqueness of the first question often disappears. The unique wondering of Hamsun's girl—wonder that it was raining—changes into the more specific and so much narrower question: "How does it rain?" Consequently the primary question seems displaced by something tangible and is entirely forgotten by the questioner. Of course, the girl's wonder was centered wholly upon those first drops of rain falling about her, and in questioning remained quite faithful to them; but it arose from the very occurrence of the rain itself. Hence it is faithful only to itself, and (given enough depth) it is objectively interchangeable: that is, interchangeable not empirically but with its omnipresent totality; not ultimately directed to that which has developed but to a question itself, passing through the world, undeveloped and unanswered. Here a fundamental question of the existent itself can be detected: one that is itself ultimately answerable only with itself, with its own individual and as yet undeveloped substance.

In contrast, all specific, particular and empirical questions are modifications of the unique impact of the basic wonder-arousing question. Admittedly, in their tangible substance they have become specific, but they are also estranged from their initial stimulus and concern. Since they become definite and, finally, concrete, their shape is adjusted to suit what is presently available and accessible; therefore it is as if (as already noted) wonder at the rain were really only an interest in the water cycle and nothing else. Thus the initial question, a veritable neophyte among questions which still has no idea at all what it really wants to know, can soon forget its own asking, and allow itself to be superseded by the offer of readily available thoughts and answers in the supermarket of things which have become what they are.

Of course nothing would be falser, nothing more misleading and even unhealthy than to separate the fundamental question from the world. As it develops, and precisely thus, wonder must be suckled wholly on outward looks, particularities, instances; must experience unflinchingly the weather of the world process, which brings with it quite different questions, quite different trials. But in all this, still undeflected, the initial amazement belongs in the questioning that has become specific. This world's great riddles should not (as I said in my *Traces*) completely hide the one straightforward mystery. And so we must take heed not only of the dreams of youth, but of simple wonder. Ultimately men are struck (often by chance) by the striking thing itself; and the thing itself first makes us take note, first makes us fore-sighted.

DIFFICULTIES

4. Too Small a Space

Wherever we go, we go too. Confined within the straits of our selves; straitened within the confines of our environment. Of course the average Philistine, your smug or blinkered citizen (usually both), occupies his hereditary place on the understanding that he can always move on. Yet his outlook is no broader from a higher point, precisely because the site and the property are all the more worth having. Everything stays out of sight and out of mind because it's different.

Our body too was originally designed for tasks simpler than the one now before it. The physical equipment we have (as they say) inherited, is restricted—and eventually often overburdened. The station hall was not built for the lark; and not for man, at whose cradle no one sang the songs of steam. Our primordial nature is inadequate when faced with these demands; inescapable, our nakedness is always there beneath the clothing of artifice. In the dawn of history these hands served to gather fruit or to wield a club, but not to play the piano. These eyes were skilled at seeking out the prey and enemies of man, but not the debris of lunar craters or the diminutive life in a drop of water. And even something clearly visible is hardly or only inadequately perceived by those who have not grown up in a

9

civilized environment. The thing seen lacks, as it were, a natural visual field in which to locate it. When something beyond these primitive physical confines is wholly incommensurate with what is known, it remains alien—not just unnoticed but literally unseen. According to Georg Forster, the Fijians reacted in this way when they were "discovered"; the boats that put out through the reefs towards the islands were seen clearly and emphatically by the natives, because they were able to match them with their own dugouts; but the big English sailing-ships that had to anchor outside the reefs were irreconcilable, and remained beyond their consciousness. A special case, yet in the wider context of perception, a mere dugout alone can restrict the visual world, making its narrowness (and ultimately the blinkers before one's eyes) all the more plain and susceptible. Even when the field of perception is extended beyond one's own physical capabilities, and beyond the circumscription of a primitive environment, the restrictive, specific locality is still there.

The solitary (should he exist) is always too used to himself. For the most part the individual man sits in the conventional boat of his environment, his class, and what is known as public opinion. The latter does not necessarily stem from his own class, but is much more frequently dispensed by the group that holds sway over it and him. The prophets of the Greek Enlightenment, the Sophists, were the first to advert to the specific restriction of the small; and above all to the inherent solitariness of the individual and his ultimate concern with the experience of self. Gorgias took this to an extreme, postulating that not just purely individual feeling but ideas of other—external—phenomena could derive from the confines of the solitary individual, whose individuality was ultimately incommunicable, even through formally communicative gestures, signs and words. Consequently the specific, individual locality cannot be communicated, even though none other can be present in experiencing and thinking about something. In fact this restricted island restricts even itself, by cutting itself off from what lies without. It separates itself from what occurs to the senses (which

10

offer neither the same things, nor all things, to all men); and divides itself from what thoughts might offer (and not all men think alike). This limitation was easily accepted, because, as circumscription, it left nothing whatsoever to be perceived apart from its own self. It might be thought of as a kind of little Philistia which only shuts in and shuts out.

How often the real Philistia—not of the individual but of the group, of the self-enclosed class and its unthinking rhetoric—has proved to be the restraint from which men have sought release, and tried to break out into true enlightenment. One of Gottfried Keller's metaphors fits the case: the dog whose snout is so thickly smeared with whey that he thinks the whole world is made of it. Relevant too are what Francis Bacon called the "Idols": the Idols of the Tribe (or anthropocentric concepts); the Idols of the cave (or personal prejudices); the Idols of the market place (or undefined terms and clichés); and the Idols of the theatre (or blindly accepted traditions. And tradition can set blinkers on a man that prevent him from seeing the world in any other way).

Our position and the restriction—indeed misrepresentation—of the outlook it afforded was not recognized for a long time. But the process of identification is by no means at an end; the surveyor's services are still required—even by those who make light of their chains.

5. *Doubt*

What begins with us stirs from us, and is never still. Ever and again it steps back to see what lies ahead; for its questioning also allows of doubt—above all of profitable doubt, when conventional and supposedly lucid explanations no longer suffice; when questioning—even if it has already been allayed—reappears, once more unsettled; or when new questions occur in the new material of the very answers themselves. Thomas Mann once said that writers are people who find writing harder than others do; it is equally true that philosophers are those who find

11

thinking harder. Especially harder than the bourgeois finds it—for he has his clichés ready; and harder than some old men who are more prompt with their opinions than even rash youth. But new observations supervene, transmitted by the senses; new associations arise, conceived and seized by the mind. Thus theories are refuted, or actually overtaken by new ones—a process that applies both to the greater subjection and poverty of the greater number, and to Newton's fixed, absolute and immutable space.

Therefore doubt is the most important stimulus of scientific progress—its prompting thorn, its spur. And the proficient learner is never a pious recipient or a mere appropriator of received ideas.

Doubting is imbued with openness of endeavor—a readiness to be tested. Hardly fortuitous, then, that as a scientific mistrust of convention it demanded a break with the taboo of hitherto received opinions. Thus philosophizing first arose and came to the fore in every nation—in Greece pre-eminently, and there with least restraint among the Sophists. But even the Sophists signified a period of development—an initiative in default of which there would have been no Socrates to establish new bases of thought; for theirs was no period of decadence characterized by lassitude rather than enthusiasm, by total doubt and nothing else. Certainly one hundred per cent doubt, cost what it may, turns advantage into calamity and proves more inimical to thought than the blindest faith: no longer the enabling spur, but only a crippling paralysis. In most cases all that separates such extreme doubt from sheer despair is its more fashionable cut; for this simple defeatism is a very easy and comfortable attitude to adopt (though of course it must be distinguished from the kind of commitment—whether purely anti-communist or anti-metaphysical—from which thought is wholly absent).

The real doubter is never so self-assured, for doubt is a thorn; and the *real* sceptic is no agnostic: he seeks to perceive, and cultivates not the theory of ignorance but the theory of knowledge. Like Faust, he is not resigned to the onset of total doubt: it is Mephistopheles who advises him to "despise all Reason and

12

all Knowledge"—the counsel of the Prince of Lies in total doubt, and not the Cartesian recommendation of fruitful doubt in all things, the better to deal with things. The counsel of the dialectic too is far from that of Mephistopheles; its scepticism is the breeze which announces the thaw (or the harrow which drives the furrow) of negation—negation which is torpor's foe but an assistant of revival. Here is the only fruitful, unhypostatized and *methodical* form of doubt, which brings about true freedom and openness; in other words, the urge born of wonder that finds no end in nihilism, but in matters of doubt new matter worthy of doubt.

To err is human, but to doubt is more human; for doubt struggles with errancy, which then falls not into error, but remains without wholly losing its way; being not scepticism that turns away from truth, but the rust (and never the gold) solvent for truth.

THE (APPARENTLY) BROKEN STICK

We feel insecure when what we see is seen indistinctly. But what is clear to our eyes we are certain—especially certain—must be so. Surprising then, that doubt arose from seeing what lay before our eyes. Its healthy mistrust was first directed against the *senses,* and only later against the intellect. Not strange then: for in this way the conventional was called in question, and what is more conventional than the serene acceptance of sensations—the most obvious support of thought itself. The stick in the stream only seems to be broken, despite the evidence of our eyes. The optical illusion is quite demonstrable. But what if the thing mobile, that we see so unmistakably, or the thing immobile (which seems much more ordinary, more "natural"), were an illusion? Zeno of Elea maintained that motion was unreal; Heraclitus that there was nothing abiding: a closer season for thought, and for its unreasonable expectation of in the one case distinctly changeless "Being," and in the other ceaseless flux.

But in any case there was a less extreme discovery: because the senses are inherently "superficial," there on the "surface" where they are wholly sense-data, the evidence of the senses must not be believed but *examined*. The illusion that the stick in the stream was broken was easily overcome by the evidence of the senses: by touch, by the credible result of passing the entire length of the stick between one's fingers. But that the sun does not really rise in the east and go down in the west, describing a circle in the sky in the process, was the ultimate paradox—the ultimate refutation of any evidence that seemed as clear as daylight. And to return to the ancient world, to Democritus (by no means inimical to the senses but one who examined their evidence): the detachment of the "truly substantial" from sound, color and from all qualities in more recent though still Democritan natural science was a decisive departure from the essential viewpoint of the senses, even though it started out from it. Galileo, and then Hobbes with the mathematical theory of motion (moving bodies as the only form of experience open to scientific observation), broke in a purely quantitative way with the "trimmings" of former sensuous appearance. Locke (otherwise far from audacious) added the theory (hardly his own unaided supposition) of the wholly secondary internal qualities, and the primary external quantities, as the limited but sole form of real knowledge. In this way the external world was entirely emptied of taste, smell, color and sound; as if an immense though ultimately doubly effective vacuum-cleaner had demonstrated its problem-solving efficiency (against which the vagaries of Goethe's *Optics* and *Chromatics* were an understandable reaction).

Now the visible world—as far as its visibleness was concerned—must itself be a gigantic optical illusion; the day could be taken as objectively illusory, being reduced and indeed confined to purely subjective perception (but of what?). These were the ultimate results of such extreme scepticism; results which not only mechanically deflated any external world, but simultaneously over-inflated the internal world qualitatively (more of which later).

14

Externality became increasingly a matter of mechanics and calculation: now color was deemed to exist only in the eye of the beholder (and in song). And of course, when that seen by the eye no longer had any external existence, *thought* (a more deeply penetrating light) became all the more responsible for what was seen; until thought's star also began to wane—but with profit.

WIND AND (TOO) LOFTY TOWERS

As I have said, it was only much later that doubt was cast upon the appropriateness of "thought" itself. For to serve its presumed purpose it must be supposed to be there in the first place, and to have done its work against purely mythical ideas. But afterwards, indeed in the very middle of the process, the testing, analytic reaction certainly came into play—and not only through a *reactionary* and flatly anti-rational effort on the part of the supporters of mythical ideas.

Admittedly, this variety of spurious and purely exploitative scepticism was also employed to the detriment of its own genuine spirit of challenge, and its clear intention to remove only the dross. Hence Luther fulminated against "that fool reason"; and—long before him—Bernard de Clairvaux (whose piety took a somewhat different form) opposed the allegedly self-abrogating mode of thought and contradiction of Peter Abelard, that shrewd dialectician of early scholastic philosophy. Simultaneously, in Islam, Al Gazali—a critic of the doctrines of Avicenna—produced his sceptical and mystical *Destructio philosophorum* (in the eleventh and twelfth centuries).

These were attempts to save belief or "faith," like Pascal's very noble effort some years later (*"l'ordre du coeur"* against, or at least above, *"l'ordre de la raison,"* in consideration of the *"faiblesse de l'esprit humain"*). There is an obvious extension of this movement in Kant's statement that he would have to "abrogate knowledge in order to make room for faith," by which of course he means only "moral faith." Kant is never more delightfully witty than when he tilts against the "architects whose sundry thoughts are built with air" and "those lofty towers . . . round which there is usually a great deal of wind"[1]; but his wit is directed against aerial, not *solid* architects—not even those who erect towers.

Ultimately, in all this, a form of genuine scepticism was implied, that was concerned precisely with the testing of knowledge for the sake of better *knowledge itself.* Although the scepticism about *thought* of a Sophist of the quality of Protagoras was genuine, it was much more important and unequivocally heuristic in the case of Socrates, for whom the new knowledge was to know nothing. Similarly, if not with Pyrrho of Elis, the head of a school of scepticism (*epochē,* or suspension of judgment) for the sake of peace of mind, then assuredly in the case of an disquietude such as that of Carneades—or the criticism of syllogistic inference to which it gave rise. Was a service was done to the theory of systematic knowledge by posing the following questions? —How can it be shown in the *conclusion* that Caius is mortal if both the *major premiss* and the *middle term* (from which the inference is to be made) already presuppose the case? Therefore how can the major premiss posit that all men are mortal, if it is not even known that Caius is mortal? How can the middle term posit that Caius is a man, if it is not even agreed whether so essential a human quality as that of being mortal is to be predicated of him?

A purification of knowledge, and the resulting room for growth, were therefore to become evident at the beginning of modern rationalistic thought: a clearing-up operation for the sake of a more rational knowledge (until the prompting thorn affected this too). Even Cartesian doubt, emerging from the old standardized school, effected a highly radical change in scepticism about thought (i.e. the preceding scholastic thought), precisely in order to obtain from this scepticism a new and apparently more genuine, adamantine *Ratio.* No more can be required of doubt than that the utterly certain should follow from the *Dubito;* and doubt would never be pressed (and even distilled) further.

Until of course this far too pure form of understanding laid itself open to attack. The new and most recent mode of doubt about thought is doubly constituted. *Firstly,* sense data are taken as more reliable and backed against thought, by a *positivism* opposed to the essential nature of thought in the sense of abstract general ideas, in accordance with Hume's arguments against the existence of such connexions in cognition (cause and effect, the concept of an externally existent body). Moreover, a similar critique was part of a respectable English tradition that universal concepts were mere *flatus vocis,* or "breath of the voice" (as they were condemned by the late-mediaeval nominalists Duns Scotus and, above all, William of Ockham). This critique reached its fullest expression in the argument for a so-called pure (i.e. exclusive) sense experience in the "empiriocriticism" of Avenarius and Mach (with, of course, a considerable reduction and underselling of Hume). But in this particular form of scepticism about the function of thought, all that remained was an economical exclusion from knowledge of ideas extraneous to the given—an adjustment of sense-perceptions; hence, for Mach, even the atom was a mere figment of thought, and therefore nothing. Most modern physicists—with the noteworthy exception of Planck—nevertheless accept this far too superficial "model" conception of thought; consequently they assent to an abstractly mathematized world that they simultaneously minister to with complete scepticism.

And so the model or experimental concept itself has *two aspects:* it means mere speculation about the relations of "facts"; but it can also mean that the world of so-called facts itself is still in a thetic, model stage in itself; that itself it still does not know which way to go, and is inherently in a constant state of trial directed to the discovery of its own true being. Accordingly, cognitive models would have to be verified, not so much—in a positivist manner—against "facts," as against (in this case) objectively real *models.* For model theory this would therefore imply both its contrary (with regard to agnosticism), and its unexpected and quite circuitously operating acceptance (regarding what is experimental and undogmatic in the known

17

object itself). Mere "cognitive experimentation" then becomes an experiment taking place not only in thoughts but in things themselves. The mere "ideal type" as, say, the model for an initial survey of the cultural-historical variety, then extends beyond the merely heuristic: and—if possible—as a still open and tendentious form (right up to the "idea") in the historical-cultural manifestations themselves. From this viewpoint, therefore, model thought (born of scepticism) becomes a fragment of anticipatory thesis, of premonitory and utopian imagination, in cognition. This aspect is now wholly without the far too forced kind of doubt that would take every element of thought, every logically connected element of appearances as being *solely fictive*—in which case there is a danger of the omission of all universal concepts, without regard to person and object. Not only of the ego and the soul, but just as much of something far less spiritual, i.e. matter. A danger too that the whole realm of connexions (rules, laws) accessible to thought would fade away to become the shadow of a merely functional relationship (if x changes, y changes; if y changes, x changes). More significantly, however, scepticism about *thought* made a contribution to epistemology in ensuring that scepticism about the senses did not become a charter for mere figments of the mind.

Enough then about the suppression of pure understanding by low-lying attacks. However, there is something very different from *positivist* doubt and its consequences: and that is *anti-idealistic* scepticism about the mind. In other words, doubt about the status of thought as an effective and substantial spiritual element in the world itself. In question here is the element tested experimentally, and imbued through analysis with quite sound distrust—something that is rather too fine, sublime, logos-like and, in short, too idealistic, to be true. With regard to history, suspicion of ideology enters in here; and as regards the world *in toto,* distrust of theology in relation to all forms of spiritual traffic in the world. Here the demolishing action of analysis, exposing and disenchanting without question in its search for the very substance of the matter, shows that this kind of scepticism is lasting *enlightenment*. Disbelief in

18

manifold surrogate ideas, primarily of the idealistic variety, led Freud to discover the much less spiritual impulses under repression. With a much more incisive instrument than disbelief, Marx revealed economic interest instead of ideas in the historical mechanism; of course with reciprocal action, but reciprocal in such a way that when an idea conflicts with an interest, it is without question the idea that is compromised. Consequently, the dialectic of the Hegelian Spirit of history was inverted precisely in this historical field, the world spirit as total demi-urge having (since Kant's *A General Natural History and Theory of the Heavens*) lost the initiative here as well. In any case, this acid of doubt, its specific *aqua fortis,* destroyed all possible hypostases of the world of thought as thoughts of the world. Admittedly, this movement was often excessive, and often without any guarantee against that quite different form of de-spiritualization, which is not enlightenment but pseudo-enlightenment; not liberalization but obstruction, stupidity, and the triumph of the banal. The fatal category of "nothing-other-than . . ." belongs in this false kind of demystification (itself enclosed in the mists); and "nothing-other-than . . ." will not permit an idea as product to appear—not *a priori*—but as a culminating product. Then not only are soap-bubbles reduced to suds, as is only right, but—with the total "nothing-other-than . . ."—gold becomes pinchbeck.

Certainly the reduction or "tracing back" of every intelligible thing to what is most alien to it, to what at best inspired it or started it off, is a form of vulgar materialism that is death to the spirit rather than a de-mister and cleansing agent for it. This cheap mephistophilism has also produced a nothing-other-than to the point of the grotesque—the following statement of Kautsky's: "Therefore the Reformation is nothing other than the ideological expression of far-reaching changes on the contemporary European wool-market." This kind of idiocy is very distant from the penetration of thought in the genuine sense of Enlightenment scepticism; in the sense of an illuminating critique of any fogging of the issue, and especially of any intellectual card-sharping. That alone has been the real office of

19

anti-idealistic scepticism and its legacy—or, as Marx puts it: "Criticism has torn away the imaginary flowers with which man's chains were decked, not in order that he should wear his chains without the comfort of illusions, but that he may throw off the chains and pluck the living flowers."[2] Or: so that he may allow thought (precisely because it is not a demi-urge) its truly illuminating function as the light that shines out ahead in this world, which is divided into the inner world still replete with thoughts, and the exterior world still not wholly reconciled with it. Wherefore the contemplation of both spheres—that of the consciousness and that which is relatively independent of consciousness—still requires a great deal of demystifying scepticism, so that ultimately the world may be or become more thoughtful.

6. Reciprocity of the Inner and Outer Worlds; Union

How simple it seems—man seated within himself, peering out. The "I" dwells within, encased in the skin (that would not otherwise, as one's "own skin," be so commonly made synonymous with one's own life). Beyond that skin, in what is therefore known as "outside," things have their dwelling-place: in a space where we are not, and through which we always pass as if mere visitants, stretching out our hands to engage with it. But when the individual, the subject that passes thus through the outside world, tries to contemplate itself, it is hazy even to itself —merely neutral and not objective. Just as one's head, right down to the shoulders, is wholly missing when one looks at oneself (like some kind of void in the self-contemplated "I"), so our being-our-self is, as we know well, altogether hazy and missing from the totality of every clearly visible environment. This is the case too when one is heavily involved in a situation— when it is visually more obvious and more pertinent to the subject. Hence the sense of something unrecognizable when a lover looks at a snapshot of himself and his girl-friend (or even when a speaker is shown one of himself addressing a meeting)— although, optically, he sees what everyone else sees: himself as

20

others saw him (the others who likewise did not then see themselves). Of course this does not exclude the possibility that the owner of this interior self is particularly concerned more with himself than with the "you" and the "it" outside himself.

There is, of course, variation in what only the inner world will have stressed from the start. A psychological distinction may even now be made between the so-called "introvert" and "extravert." Either can appear together with the egotistical and the more altruistic type, yet these volitional moral elements are not the distinguishing factors. Among the introverted there are some very orderly (even indeed, far too bland) natures; and not all extraverts—the objectively oriented—are by any means good men (but more often cold by nature). The distinction is just as far from being synonymous with that made between so-called "emotional" and so-called "matter-of-fact" people; and also coincides only approximately (at least not objectively) with the well-known and often tritely expressed differentiation of the sexes. Youth is more substantial, of course—the kind represented by Goethe's *Werther*,[3] that is; and the young people of *Torquato Tasso*[4] are introverted in a unique way, in spite of their being together—which is in itself their isolation. Whereas extraversion may be substantially proper to manhood (when man's estate may be to survey the world round about him)—not only to the manhood of the practical Antonio (as against the poet Tasso), but *expressis verbis* to the theme of *Wilhelm Meister*[5] as the novel about education—about growing towards *objectivity* (with a definitely existing subject, far removed from Werner, the dry conformist Philistine). Here extraversion can go so far that, as when a living-room is furnished, ornaments are arranged against the objective walls that stand a certain distance away, whereas the subjective chairs and sofa which lie more to the center of the space are ignored; but beyond this caricature, a capacity for organizing space and producing things is the distinctive mark of extraversion. Above all both kinds of attitude are found in thinkers, seldom quite unalloyed, but nevertheless with a recognizable preponderance of extraversion or introversion in the mixture.

The antitheses of Kierkegaard and Hegel—with a certain refinement for argument's sake—are apt here (not Hegel entire, and certainly not the Hegel of the *Phenomenology of Spirit,* but the Hegel adduced as typical by Kierkegaard). "What there is of me in my philosophy," said Hegel, "is false." And conversely, Kierkegaard, the advocate of "understanding oneself in existence" and of self-examination, might have said: "Whatever in my philosophy is *not* of me, is false; subjectivity alone is certain truth." Of course modern so-called "existentialism" does not go so far—at least not the psychologically tempered version that we find, say, in Jaspers. Equally, in modern times the purely objective structure is met with only in mere imitations, as for instance in Nicolai Hartmann's copies of Hegelian and especially Aristotelian "classifications"; his *extra muros* is all the more recognizable because of its impersonal approach. And it occurs in a thoroughly reduced and mechanical-materialistic form where the no longer expressed but only alienated picture of the world is so large and at the same time so small that there is no longer any room in it for even a head. In short: negatively, the introverted and the extraverted show themselves, in the one case, as something evaporating, and, in the other, as something dying away; and positively, in the one case, in transcendental meditation, and, in the other, in a substantial view of the world. There is an often ambivalent friction between inwardness and the content of the aphoristic couplet that closes Gottfried Keller's *Song at Nightfall:* "Drink, O eyes, as much as lashes hold,/ Of this world's plenteous overflowing gold"—but also between St. Jerome in his study,[6] and the starry heavens.[7]

THE CONSTANT, HABITUAL COMMERCE
BETWEEN THEM

That man is seated within himself, looking out, is a simple observation that dawns on one quite early in life. Of course, children do not take it that way only, even when they realize that they are "I"s. They do not just look out at things, but things look at them: the water winks at them with its water-eyes, and the cupboard spies them as they pass; it can be very frightening. And if we try to grasp something with too smooth a surface, the polished part seems unfriendly and rejects our grip, whereas something fashioned in another way, something which is graspable, places itself in the enclosing hand. To this extent, what is within is not only named and christened from without, but with regard to the affections also endows the outside with speech—much less often, yet much more individually; as with the emotional tonality of colors, phenomena that are exclusively without, and not intrinsic to man's inner being. Red, yellow, green, blue, violet; so-called harmonic "tones" are associated with and seem inescapably to adhere to specific colours, which in their turn are inevitably attached to specific objects. An impression gained thus would not be experienced without this constant reciprocal movement. The glitter of jewellery and the variegated effects of gems are similarly produced. How often this added shimmer has enhanced a woman's radiance, or added the crowning touch to the aura of monarchy. But how? The barrier between within and without is not impervious but porous. It operates even when the gaiety proper to the child is long gone: for instance, in the very mature observation that one can see only those in the light, not those in darkness[8]—with its ambiguous reference to the obscurity of the lower depths and the elevation of public office. This too means a looking back: the unseen itself, or abandonment; that which is seen too much, or manufactured fame. In such things, "within" and "without" are still mixed, though not impurely from the start.

EMPATHY—STILL WITHOUT CLEAR DEFINITION OF "I" AND "NOT-I"

Therefore the apparently so simple "within" or "without" is just as little the sole source of direct experience as this reciprocity implies. An earlier discovery precedes and lingers after that of the skin as our wall, and the eyes as a window. This

23

earlier and unfading discovery is doubtless more cloudy than the clear-cut impact of the skin and the eye; yet it offers its own kind of illumination. And the dimness is not in its very action, but is more precisely described as an emotionally penetrating haziness—as *empathy*. In this a certain opening up and unlocking seems to take place, to the extent that something that is otherwise external is not just sensed, or perceived through the senses, but, one might say, felt-into, and itself so harmonized with man that it looks back at him. The impression is therefore human—all too human—and yet inevitable: the lake "smiles," the wind "moans" (its moaning is not merely "long-drawn out," but "lonely"), and the pillar "pushes up" or even "aspires" towards the heavens. (Theodor Lipps was very much concerned with such phenomena, but unfortunately only as a psychologist. Nevertheless his studies did reveal the peculiar process of empathy, as when joy is "felt out" of a dog's wagging its tail.)

Not only poetic but everyday language is full of such long-established empathies. Their hither-thither/thither-hither quality is a feature of language from the most banal advertising-copy ("This film is one uproarious whirl of spice and gaiety—*and* it's got all those blue-sky and fleecy-cloud moments too") to "the pure clouds' unhoped-for blue"[9] of the poet. It is long-established because still touched with a fair amount of atavism and animism; of course, this quality does not allow empathy any solidity, but rather demands constant scrutiny. Nevertheless, *mutatis mutandis,* when the insight is scrutinized it is possible to see how the assertion that the sky is "cheerful" or "serene" can persist alongside the more straightforward statement that the sun "rises in the East." For the figuratively assigned serenity could always refer to some qualitative aspect of the sky—say to a day in May—obviously not literally but transparently; whereas a rising (or going-down) of the sun does not really occur in any case. In addition, a counter-movement (or, more exactly, a retrograde movement) is characteristic of the hither-thither/without-within transference of language (i.e., say, "hardness" for a character, "illumination" in the sense of enlightenment for an epoch, and so on). A man is described as "open" as if he

24

were a wardrobe; yet Keller in one of his stories describes a wardrobe as "patriarchal," as if it were a man of such disposition. This kind of induced empathy extends from the gay or gaily murmuring Schubertian stream to the sublime lines from the *Walpurgisnacht* scene of Goethe's *Faust* (lines charged with Goethe's objectivity): "An imperfect disk, a tardy-glowing light,/ How sickly-sad the red moon rises on the night."[10]

Significantly these verses gain their effect because it is possible here for the anthropomorphic interjection of "sickly-sad," and of "imperfect," to stand without any noticeable fracture next to purely physical descriptive terms such as "glowing light" and "red moon." In Wilde's *Salomé,* the guilty Herodias seeks to wash her hands of actuality when she says: "*La lune ressemble à la lune, c'est tout. Rentrons . . .*" (The moon is just the moon—let us retire).

But no empathy allows any retiring in place of emergence from self and going out with evident compulsion into what is otherwise alien. Indeed, the pillar aspires to the heavens only as an extension of our own limb, and when the wind's chromatic tones make their melancholy sound, they do so only to express our own disquietude. But where in our self-extension is the something which, by analogy, as it were, *felt* the empathy—the feeling of sadness—*into* the tardy-glowing moon, and especially into the active aspect of its ascent? And finally, with regard to analogy itself (which is obviously not an emotional transition, but a reasoning process), where in the lightning-fast and inevitable act of empathy is there time and place for predication *per analogiam* (inferring the sighing of the wind from the content of one's own sighs) to be exercised? Surely it is easier to suppose that in the process of empathy there is a precedent feeling-in and feeling-out, which humanizes to a considerable extent, but certainly not thoroughly and above all not at the deeper levels of the content it has before it for conversion. Of course there are pre-logical operations, but to consider them is not pre-logical—as little as their so tenaciously sustained, and not wholly subjectively grounded compulsion. Rather, it may be said that empathy is still the most habitually frequented

25

bridge between the "within" that is felt, and the "without" that is simply sensed.

THE INCREASED CLARITY OF "I" AND "NOT-I"; A RELATIONSHIP THAT BECOMES PRECARIOUS

This duality has never been divided for long, and never continuously. And there is a very significant primordial tide that moves in a state much more precarious than and quite different from the process of empathy. As a warning, and also in thanksgiving for the lucidity of the "within" on the one hand, and the "without" on the other, actual eruptions of atavism occur here; these are neurotic and indeed schizophrenic as well as desperate incursions between the interior and the exterior; so that subject and object appear to change places entirely. The head is the street, the street the head; the sinuous valley is the very serpent within—everything winding round and back, everything entangled. These unclarified impulses from the long past neither-nor of subject and object are so disorderly, that we are plainly faced here with a recurrence of the animistic element of primitive times: reproduced now, of course, solely as a psychological element of primitive history—i.e. of and from the not yet extant "within," and the not yet solidified "without." In a grim way, indeed, coinciding not only with an all-enlivening, but an inspiring animism. In any case, the so-called "natural view of life" or "world view" which has an unmixed subject on the one hand, and an unmixed object on the other is clearly not natural, but primarily acquired.

Above all, in the primitive state of the economically undifferentiated tribe, there was (and is) no question of any consciousness of being an "I"; therefore the ego-consciousness did not, with its since then so extraordinarily refined barrier of skin, separate itself from the outside existence of other men, and even things. Even mere schizophrenic atavisms (which are wholly un-natural nowadays) to some extent reproduce the wholly natural mixed image of man and of the world of those times.

26

The primitive knows his soul; but in such a way that he represents and names it not as an individual, but as—say—the bird flying between the trees (or some other totemic sign of the whole clan outside), in a perception of the world that is not only animalistic, but entirely bifurcated. All this changed when, with the division of labor (that is, with the education of master and servant) the master at least was able to develop an I-feeling centered in himself. And then the individual *I-consciousness itself* (which today seems almost to be something inherited physiologically) arose for the first time as an amazingly new phenomenon in societies that were no longer tribal (but also no longer despotic and indeed not confined within their own bounds): that is, in the Greek merchant states, and then preeminently—and with a more acute emphasis thereafter—in the Renaissance.

The Greeks, reputedly so outward-looking, were also the first to react to being an *I*. Not only by reason of the great number of visible individuals among them for whom the world appeared in unconventional forms, but above all because, on reflection, they distinguished self-consciousness by name in addition to consciousness. Aristotle and Plotinus had to be born before something so proper to the ego as the "hearing of hearing" (*akuein tu akuein*) and a "conscious knowledge of self" (*parakoluthein heautō, syneidēsis*) could be reflected and become central. Of course, it was already preceded by something sharply defined—the selfness of the Sophists, the "know yourself" and Socrates' reaction, and the Epicurean and stoical recourse to privacy, right up to "self-contemplation" or meditation (*Ta Eis Heauton*) with Marcus Aurelius. And what a powerful new effect (and after-effect) was exerted from a quite different point (from the Bible) by that explicit and emphatic call: *Salva animam meam* ("Save my soul . . ."). Exerted right up to the full birth of the "I" in the newly discovered "inwardness" of Augustine, and consciousness of self as the prior certainty. Now we have the incomparably full and deep self-analyses of Augustine's *Confessions;* the extreme cries of the "I"; the calling out of inwardness, with a flexion from and to

God himself. Hence Augustine's sayings: "Do not go outwards; the truth dwells within you" (*in te interiore*), and "I would know God and my soul, and nothing else—nothing else at all." From here the watchword went forward to mediaeval mysticism —and pre-eminently the introverted transcendent variety. *Te interiore* was the slogan for Meister Eckhart's recommendation to be the image and likeness of God himself and God alone; the fiery "spark," the "fortress," "the depth of his own indwelling" —"*synderesis*" (or spark of conscience) without any "otherness" of an object.

From Augustine onwards, various degrees of self-examination were conceived of, in which the *Christian self* (and by no means the *creaturely ego*) enjoyed pre-eminence. But this primacy disappeared under the influence of quite unspiritual, extremely worldly currents extending far into modern bourgeois times. Even the *Renaissance* brought a methodical-rational conception to bear instead of the spiritual-visionary probing of inwardness; its subject was transcend*ental,* not transcend*ent* contemplation —beginning with the *Dubito, cogito, ergo sum.* "I am, therefore God is, therefore the world is" (*Ego sum, ergo est deus, ergo est mundus*), with Descartes; and "God is, therefore the world is, therefore I am" (*Deus est, ergo est mundus, ergo ego sum*) with Thomas Aquinas—what a difference in the capacity and eminence of the subject! And, very far from natural, so played and forced up at this point—with the certainty of the subject and uncertainty of the object—there arose the precarious subjéct-*object* relationship. The egress of the subject was now also posited epistemologically for the first time; and from that beginning, after Hume, the prompting spur of epistemology—the theory of knowledge—made a radical entry into the world, with a radical form of self-reflection in the case of Kant. "I believe that to be a necessary accompaniment of all my ideas," said Kant; according to his theory, thought was no longer in passive representation, but in all *production*—i.e. of forms, uniquely generated by the subject, through which objective knowledge comes. Here, of course, the subject (with which Kant's radical "Copernican revolution" is concerned, so that the understanding does not depend upon things, but things do depend upon the understanding) is not the individual subject, but is said to be wholly a "consciousness-in-general," or a purely logical and necessarily valid universal consciousness (*Bewusstsein über-haupt*). In this way precisely it is stressed as a universal *sphere,* and therefore for the first time established over and above the hitherto unique sphere of the world that was held to be independent of the consciousness.

And so, with a massive acceptance of the Socratic "know yourself," the concept of the knowledge of things moved back to a penetratingly analyzed *knowledge of the knowledge* of things: that is, to that *a priori* before all intellectual experience which first establishes such experience as intellectual. To, accordingly, the "transcendental method"; the transcendental nature of the highest (i.e. the most profound) introversion, in contrast to all transcendence and anything transcendent to the consciousness—whether as a mundane thing-in-itself, or as a world above. But of course that which uniquely establishes and substantiates in this way is the power of the transcendental *a priori* as against the merely empirically assembled *a posteriori* that appears to be given and present externally. This power would then arise solely from the spontaneity (the generative power) of the transcendentally discovered subject; and therefore of the same subject that is asserted not only in the *Critique of Pure Theoretical Reason,* but also in *The Critique of Pure Practical Reason,* indeed in *The Critique of Judgment,* as autonomy of the moral will, and as artistic autonomy of the creative genius which itself is the prime law-giver, and itself first posits rules. Freedom, which determines itself through itself alone, thus becomes the *sense of value* in the prevalence of the transcendental subject—from start to finish. This activity (which is not only theoretically productive) prevails above all with Fichte, for whom the "I"—the ego—generates the world of the "Not-I"—the non-ego—only in order to extend the world of representations of physical objects as a moral activity in accordance with the fundamental principle of morality. The transcendental withdrawal into the subject—this absolute "self-

29

reflection of the positing ego"—therefore becomes practical-moral projection into the world: into that which is not given but propounded to us. In Fichte's world this is solely "the material materialized for man's duty" (for the fulfillment of his moral vocation)—generated by the theoretical "I" only so that the practical "I" can prove itself on it, and prevail in it. This is a conclusive union of the self and the "world of appearance," but (and this is especially clear in Fichte's case) at a price: that which was objective became increasingly less mundane, as the massive individuality, the not merely not-I being of "Nature," was wholly excluded from mediations. But the ever more intensively elaborated pole of the self had revealed a now inalienable richness to its discoverers. The imminent result—as a consequence of capitalist alienation (of the self and the world)—was that the initially over-spiritualized subject entered in more and more, and the transcendentally and idealistically devitalized object retreated in an increasingly mechanistic fashion.

Hegel's phenomenology and system, concerned as fully with the subject as with the object (in contrast to Fichte, but in common with the Goethean system and with Schelling), a dialectics which constantly mediates between the two poles (the dialectics therefore of a mutual dispersion), was the final but also the forward-moving one in the separation of subject and object in modern idealism.

From this point on, the *unreflected* affective union, from empathy upwards, was definitely revealed as a still primitive form (*unio affectiva*).

HUMAN SELF-ALIENATION—MECHANISTIC ALIENATION OF THE WORLD ITSELF; REMEDY

The "I" and the exterior are now separated, but have also become reciprocally bleaker. The product has got beyond the control of the productive "I," and appears as a fully automatic device; everything else seems to proceed of its own accord. The social ground of these alienations is the transformation of all men and things into commodities. The analogy of a poorly comprehended and controlled circulation of commodities is largely valid as the model for a fully quantified relationship (or rather what is no longer a relationship) of objects. Above all, a socially alienated objective being (an industry or organization) can itself automatically condition an alienated subject, which, in its turn, reciprocates with external alienation. Then society, right up to and just short of the upper subjects, consists of cogs in a production-line; those above enjoying their relative freedom of action only in the interstices of the machine—or rather, as Lukács says, according to the mere chances of economic life. In this way, since the middle of the last century, the subject (theoretically too) has in general been well behind the proud *homo faber,* the *sum, ergo est mundus,* and the autonomous consciousness.

Taine's *milieu* theory, according to which men are in every case no more than reflections of their social and geographical environment, would not have been conceivable in this particular form in a previous age. Not even for the French materialists of the eighteenth century, who would allow only that physical and not social existence determined the nature of consciousness. Therefore, even in the most highly nuanced case, the individual (according to the school of Taine) ranks only as the point of intersection of social relations, and essentially as one moulded by them. Accordingly, the appropriate conjunction for statements about the relation of the individual is "because" and not "despite." There is of course an apparent similarity though not synonymity between Taine's judgment and Marx's statement that "it is not the consciousness of human beings which determines their existence, but social existence which determines their consciousness,"[11] the consciousness of the subject being only a version of its particular class-ideology.

However, precisely what Marx's emphasis on this kind of external existence does not have in common with passive *milieu* theory is its very passivity, for Marx saw the consciousness itself as a co-determinant participating in the social existence that

31

supports and determines it. Therefore: "If (social) conditions form men, then (social) conditions must be humanly formed" is not so much a requirement of the economic-social conception of history, as a firm demand of humanistic revolution (and a subjective factor *a limine* first makes the revolution possible). Already operative here was the recognition of *homo faber*—of the man who does not endure his environment with a subjective consciousness made of wax, but actively enters into it (anticipated in idealism as Fichte's transition from the postulating of thought to engagement in action). But this effect of the subject on the object does not occur in an idealistic and abstract manner, and does not proceed from the still alienated subject to an objective world in a mere mechanistic reflex-operation. Rather it is characteristic of the real, new subject-object relationship that there should be, first, an *analytical* inspection of all alienations, and ultimately objectifications, which are connected with the circulation of commodities; and, then, a *constructive* theory of the object-world (involving an expert knowledge of matter, tendency and laws), by which a real engagement may be made with the world of objects so that it can then be conditionally humanized. Therefore, despite the theoretical key and the practical lever of the subjective factor, through expertise an excess weight is clearly revealed in the objectively determinant existence which is present apart from the subject, though not independent of it *a limine* and *usque ad finem*.

Expertise in the matter itself implies a cancellation of anything within the subject that might not concern the matter in question. But no perception would be objective that did not confront human coloring as carefully as objective objectifications. All the more since these objectifications have a human, and in this case inter-human, social root. But in an attempt to be purely objective in the approach to actual objective being, the necessary removal of what pertains to the subject was certainly also taken too far—above all in the pertinent manifestations of bourgeois philosophy, because there it appeared mainly as a process of observation. Hence Külpe, the nineteenth-century advocate of an individual scientific procedure that he called "realization" (*Realizierung*), offered an entirely a-subjective characterization of the cognition of objects (clearly making psychology an objective science). According to "realization," the criterion of "real scientific" cognition is "non-dependence on the experiencing and conceiving subject." Independence of the *experiencing* subject would guarantee the qualitative-true thought process of natural science; independence of the *conceiving* subject would guarantee value-free historical and intellectual science. (In the case of this last criterion Ranke's intention is quite typical: he wanted impartially to establish the facts—"that which is"—without assuming the lofty office of a universal judge. In addition, Max Weber's would-be non-partisan and above all unemotional concept of the objectivity of social-scientific knowledge stressed science as a necessarily a-subjective calling). Of course it is clear that this kind of a-subjective attitude is, or was, very much of its time because of its correspondence to the considerably intensified systematization of the individual consciousness. So that the criterion referred to, instead of being really a-subjective, and inferring the absence of a subject (a self), in fact implies the increasingly alienated subject of entrepreneurial industrial society. And the same criterion is just as inadequate as a guarantee of any introjection-free and thus unbiased knowledge of "things as they are," for it guarantees only the already apparent de-spiritualization of the world of objects, an intrinsically fetishistic production process in which the producer but not the product is out of mind. Such a cancellation of the subject (at least in its bourgeois version) did not offer a correct forecast of the result of the process: i.e. a dead world prospect, and therefore an object-world consisting of nothing other than matter in mechanical motion; boundless, but at the same time so small that not even a single human head would find a place in it. Admittedly, even in this most extreme object-existence, there was once a very positive social levelling and commitment—i.e. still bourgeois-revolutionary. Even mechanistic eighteenth-century materialism was directed not so much against the subject *qua* subject, as against its alliance with transcendence, as the arsenal of the

33

divine right of kings (a doctrine under siege) and its Church.

From the time of this struggle onwards, materialism remained just as much (or became again) the *opposite* of object-fetishism, for it firmly denounced fetishism and analyzed it theoretically; not mechanistically, in an emptying of the world that would itself be highly fetishistic, but precisely in firm dependence on the experiencing and apprehending subject: an "explanation of the world from itself" that implies not *passive contemplation,* but the *revelation of that which produces.* Precisely this *non-effacement* of our very subject side (i.e. of its *impelling and utopian-open essence*) guarantees the cognitive elective relationship with that very truly actual essence in what is becoming, producing, qualifying and even changeable in the world, whose conscious part we are—its most advanced post. There is no such elective affinity with what has become fixed: that is, with an objective-fetishism that reveals itself ultimately as a blatant fetishism of having become and of facts; one most accurately characterized by the effacement of the subject (without any question of a differentiation and close examination of its "introjections"), leaving nothing but a dead world and ultimately a world of nihilism.

This world is then opposed to our common concerns not merely as something contrary but as that which is wholly disparate; instead of a possible "meaning" in making, we are confronted with a totally alienated, non-mediable being-in-itself—none other than the "absurd." Such are the remarkably distinct and decisive consequences of a total consideration of the object without man: the unmediated object-world round about unmediated, lonely and silent man.

It is singular, nevertheless, that both within and without are increasingly required to suggest themselves unilaterally. This was still remote from (or again departed from) classical German philosophy after Fichte; the young Schelling, for example, did not hold such a view in his "sincere youthful philosophy" (Marx), when he demanded that the producer should not be forgotten in favor of the product. For Schelling, not history but Nature was conceived of as a world in becoming, rising from slumber—in tune with the extremely objective Goethe's abundant concern with the external world. Hegel introduced the true *objectivity* as that of a permanent dialectical subject-object relationship, by virtue of the *movement* already there before man, and human-historical *work* in and on the process. Formation, transformation; a reciprocally ascending interpenetration of subject and object in which the contributions of the subjective and objective portions in the world of process were oscillating. From Hegel onwards, and primarily as a result of the active influence of his work, the omission of the subjective element from knowledge of the world, and especially from percipient transformation of the world, had no scientific standing and function other than to *sensitize* the subjective to the whole—not only in the abrogation of the ego, but just as much in the stressing of the ego; and other than to *set this stress to rights* again, as an emphasis that must be put—in rejection of any depreciation of the subject and against object-fetishism—on the power of that which is intrinsically human to open and disclose the world. For if the percipient subject is the key—and the only key—that will unlock the closed world (or rather that world which is still very much closed to itself, still very much enclosed in the depths), then the greatest critical care is required so that the key may be held, and indeed first of all moulded, methodically and appropriately.

Here the transparent subjectivity of a-subjective, so-called positivism now finds realization; and the stressed value of the subjective-factor in cognition has to make good precisely in the world of objects which is thereby disclosed and ultimately mediated to the subject. Therefore (in Fichtean terms) the primacy of practical reason, in logic as well, demands wholly and solely, independence from everything that is merely private in subjectivity, and from all prejudgments and false evidences of an unanalyzed and particular or transient interest and its restricted viewpoint. Cognition takes place not out of self-cultivation or for the sake of a so-called *Weltanschauung* psychology, but with *in-formatio* about the world and of the world itself as the goal. Indeed, the truly mysterious way does not so much lead within (as Novalis says), but *without;* ultimately it is not merely extended, but extended in depth as it strives towards the exterior.

That which is within is and remains the key to that which is without; yet the key is not the substance, but the substance of the key as well is in the object-house (as yet hardly on its way to completion) that is the world. Cognition has a function and a mission—an office—in the world such as nothing else in the world. It is not possible to conceive of this kind of unlocking and disclosing power in too outward a fashion (in a way which allows too much concern for the object), if it is not to fall into the Quixotic state of human fancy and delusion, or to return to mere idolatry of the self, with nothing before and nothing to follow. Hence more is needed than an objective turning and casting of the subjective factor into the external event, as if in obedience to the negative key line from Faust: "But they'll not raise the bolt—your wards so finely wrought."[12] Although this warning is effective if directed against mere subjective *intricacy,* it does not apply to a subject which is concerned with the object, and whose whole glory and mission is to open and indeed to be not just a key—but a veritable ignition key. Similarly, the object with its bolt is—as such—as clearly designed for the key, as the key for it; if, instead, it is directed towards a state of being-in-itself that cannot be mediated with the subjective factor, then the object too will end in nihilism. Therefore it requires a wholly objective turning in and casting out of the subject into the continuing process of the exterior: mediated and overhauled together, in accordance with a *fieri* and not a mere *factum-est* in the undecided process-existence of the world, the advance-guard of which is man, and not a fixed being-in-itself. This fully open subject-object relationship, which points to a possible mutual exchange of countenance, remains logically a frontier notion, and metaphysically a frontier ideal. This reciprocity has—in a straightforward and appropriately utopian fashion—been characterized as an external self-encounter "by virtue of which that which is inward can become outward, and that which is outward can become as that which is inward" (*Spirit of Utopia,* 1923). This, however, presupposes continuous inspection of the inward movement (tested against the tendential course of external things), and of the outward movement (measured according to its approximation to the as yet unextracted though latent interior and center of the world).

"Embark!" was Nietzsche's ultimate summons: and the voyage through the outside world, especially to new waters, has always been one on which the discoverer went himself, afterwards being intimately associated with what was discovered. Ultimately, therefore, so that within and without might have reciprocal good fortune, every incursion into the subject was concomitant with the rise of its appropriately conformable world —a process that did not have to wait for Hegel's *Phenomenology of Spirit.* And the power to effect the within and not to abandon the without is an effective power only for a phenomenology of the way home that does not appease the world as already given.

THE JOURNEY:
METHOD AND MOTIVE

7. Probing

"Think it over!"—more easily said than done. To commune with, to enter into oneself, is all the more difficult a task because the outlet gives so little clearance for the run-in. Of course that doesn't prevent one sinking into thought. Only the stagnant and obdurate stay motionless.

Entering into oneself means keeping going all the time. The inner meditation that obviously does not proceed from within, moves on. But if its spirit is particularly weak and unprepared, it merely lashes out ineffectually. This is the case with concerns which are particularly close to one and thus weigh one down— to get any further, advice must be sought from another. But since acute meditation sets the meditator in motion, it also makes progress if it keeps a hold on itself and perseveres thus. This last is especially true of the kind of thinking that tests the ground it stands on. Indeed, stirring yet staying put is characteristic of that looking-back-to-itself, that temporally probing variety of meditation which penetrates below its what-has-become in order to allow it once more to come to be; this far-ranging form of recollection is not static but highly mobile— an epic disembarkation: a revelation.

Every recollection therefore moves consciously along a bore—a downwards-pointing shaft in which it sinks and rises vertically. Although it refuses to leave its position to turn either to the right or to the left, it doesn't stay in one place, but travels out vertically as well, into its "ahead" and its "wherefore," without leaving it, but also without resting in it in a twilight or subdued state. The form of thought in which one becomes immersed—in order to be such—must always have travelled in the way proper to it.

Understanding oneself employs a narrative mode; it looks back. Consequently self-comprehension displays itself as the apparent (though seldom actual) noteworthiness of an *individual* life-history, recalled from below. For instance, an old man might pick up again some coat effectively worn in the past, some played-out "once-it-was-something," and thus achieve a momentary importance. But when the looking back is recollection in motion, something that has been used very little—something that was not *put to use* at all at the time—is made to bloom. This is a more effective recall than an actual visit to the scenes of the past, for the return made in writing keeps its distance. It stays in a kind of Pullman carriage, whereas the direct "here-again" is mere return and re-flection, being far too close to what is revisited. The writer, on the other hand, as the book-keeper of his own life in retrospect, can enhance the past if his journey back is a confession—or at any rate effectively a confession—for he makes his revelation with a postdated longing for rectitude. This happens with the relentless *ad me ipsum* of life-histories that not only narrate but mercilessly stir up the memories narrated *and* the narrator himself. Hence the autobiographies of Augustine and Rousseau are actually called "Confessions," being admissions made before the judgment seat of the self. Vanity is undoubtedly a great help—a kind of intermittent support or relay station for the kind of journey back where revelations are made in stages. Almost all the best autobiographers (even the contrite) have read about "great men" in Plutarch's *Lives*. The filter of pride—as well as of vanity—is applied; and Nietzsche is not the only one to point out that memory gives way before pride: even Christian memory on the verge of repentance, marking time on the spot yet driving downwards, veritably that form of memory that would allow us to shine, even at this point, in order to grow—and to come to be.

Georg Brandes says somewhere that there are three kinds of memoirs: the Augustinian, the Rousseauian, and the Goethean. Augustine showed humility, and how he was raised up from all his confusions; Rousseau demonstrated (and stressed) how often he had stumbled; but Olympian Goethe sang his own praises, and made himself into a work of art. And there is a fourth variety, without either confessions or boasting: the journey into time lost, where the self (as in the case of Proust) apparently will not survive, and is obviously looking back from the protracted hour of its death. In this case he who remembers looks back as only the man about to depart can look back; as a revenant visualizing himself where he once was. On the other hand, the quest for the "ahead," which means a formative seeking out that is itself in motion, does not destroy the writer's self when it makes an autobiographical journey down the stages of its self-formation; when (especially in the growing-up novel) it is shown how the self-contemplator has made himself what he is. And the writer who travels into himself still moves ahead simultaneously—as when he refuses to immerse himself in any private experiences unless they are the hardly private experiences of self-formation itself, and therefore of education. Clearly, one might say that Hegel's *Phenomenology* verges on being an actual life-history; for it is a biography of human consciousness in general: how it has made itself what it is, and educated itself. Probing can have as profound a result as this only when the original goal of those travelling back is self-understanding.

The "wherefore" that must be entered into is different to the "ahead." In the case of the "ahead" only the consciousness reflects as it narrates, whereas the understanding does so in the real probing and penetration, in a remarkably lonely (i.e. world-less) attempt to get to the bottom of thought. It is lonely even when conversation with another person is employed to that end, for example by Socrates—the thinker discoursing in the market-place. For in this case the stroll and discussion do not dispense with what concerns us alone; as Socrates says, there is nothing to be learnt from the trees, but a lot can be discovered from men in the city. What is just? What is virtue? These and related questions are continually posed on the spot and penetratingly examined. Socrates, who "over and over again seems to say the same things in the same words, so that any ignorant person is sure to scoff at what he says,"[13] in fact is speaking good sense, rendering over and over again an account of the same Good. As Arnold Metzger has rightly emphasized, "his quest for the Good, which is always the same question" returns and reflects back on itself. The ignorant become conscious that what they knew has been refuted, and hence that their consciousness has deceived itself. Everything further that is to the point, while moving "transcendentally" *behind* its point, lives and moves from the basis of the Socratic reflection of understanding. It does not skim over thought, but on the contrary moves itself relentlessly into thought; which is a prerequisite of proficient thinking. Going backwards into the "wherefore" which establishes valid *a priori* knowledge is for Kant, as for Fichte, the process of self-reflection pure and simple. Indeed, at the start of this path to an unconditioned beginning, Fichte offers not a proposition (which would first of all have to be established itself) but a command: "Think yourself!" (posit your own being)—which is clearly intended as marching orders for an incursion into nothing but generative movement, taking nothing for granted, arranging everything *a priori,* developing itself. Although this command would ask too much of pure thought, as if all experience outside it were basically only its own memories, ungenetic and turned back on themselves, even here there is an unmistakable movement *en route*—even if only into itself: a getting going of going, a swimming out of water—yet no resting upon a bed of ease. Meditation that recurs and continues anew every time doesn't strike against itself all the time. There are already too many paths to take for that to happen; although sinuous, they lie open, and into their openness entries are made.

8. The Journey that is Knowing; the "Faust" Itinerary. The Walk

A man takes himself along when he goes out for a walk. Still, he does get outside himself by enriching himself with the fields, woods and mountains of his wanderings. He also learns to recognize the right and the wrong ways; and the house that takes him in at the end of his journeying is never an obvious haven, but a goal attained.

The analogy between a journey and the step by step ascent to a goal, is old, popular and instructive. Countless headmasters have trotted it out for school-leavers, suitably embellished and put to some moral end; they remark how, when the traveller looks back from the goal he has reached, once again, in quick review, he travels back over the ground he has already covered.

And so journeying is like the historical process itself, both in the history looked back on, and, above all, in the succession of events which lie ahead. Schiller's poem *The Walk*[14] provides an excellent illustration of this in its accessible though historically just and perceptive images. The road through the countryside is also a guide-path into history, which has formed and transformed these sights. The meadow, the forest and the idyllic valley come into view; then the city, and with it the image of Greek civilization. The sequel is powerful, though—as often happens with Schiller—subject to a certain petty-bourgeois restriction; yet one receives the impression of an uncompleted design: the sense of a journeying that sees, superimposed on its own progress, the succession of things that have happened.

THE "FAUST" JOURNEY

A poor traveller is a man who remains unchanged by his travels. He changes his location, without adapting himself to it or changing with it. But all the more a man is in need of determining, through experience, who and what he is, the more profoundly (and not only extensively) he will be set right by outward experience. This was the advice for the journey that Goethe offered (and the road he took) in *Wilhelm Meister,* which is a novel about the "apprenticeship" or education of Wilhelm. It was with the same design that Faust used the magic cloak which bore him out of the confined space of his own room and through such different landscapes.

The Faust who is so restless when at his studies, is (to date) the most powerfully portrayed subject of human striving and travelling towards a something that changes and fulfills. Auerbach's cellar, Faust's love for Gretchen, the Imperial Palace and Helen of Troy, become his posting-stations on the way to the most sublime moment that can truly be addressed with the words: "Stay, you are so beautiful!" And as Faust renews and adjusts himself at each stage of the journey, so what has been ex-perienced on the way appears in the reciprocal subject-object relationship as a more distantly or more closely corresponding antitype of what lies within. But only by means of man in the wind of his journeying, and by means of the world as experience in transit, does the answer dawn: "A step into the infinite is your design,/ So follow, in the finite, each and every line," and, just as much in accord with the basic intention: "Thus, in a wooden stage's narrow space,/ Through creation's sphere entire pace."[15]

Here there is no "lying on a bed of ease" masquerading as real fulfillment. Mephistopheles, as acid and drawing down, is the same as Faust, as fire and irrepressible flaming upwards; for both acid and fire consume. Mephistopheles is the maliciously deflating sneer at all achievement; but Faust is the relativization of achievement to and its transformation into a climax in which everything transient turns increasingly into a parable—right up to the as yet unexecuted, merely symbolically significant leap, after which the "inadequate"—in the utopian "here and now," in the utopian present—"becomes actual."[16] Faust's magic journey through the "whole that has become so valuable" (to

43

him) towards the moment of fulfillment, is accordingly the way in which spirit (a mind) consciously examines and adjusts all its exuberance, and also elucidates and illuminates the mere dream of a something in the world. Hence Faust (or the canonical student Goethe) travels towards the moment in which he will "know himself in a good sense," and, by virtue of his "ideal striving after his influence and empathy in nature as a whole," no longer encounters any object that would not again be set in action; that would not once more, in all its power and beauty, afford individuality an intensive "meaning." Ever and again new affliction and new hope reveal the beginning of a new sphere to unsatisfied man (as the one heedful of individuality and particularity). That is: a new level of the subject for mediation of the subject with the object, and of the object with the subject. This mediated subject-object relationship is the process of refreshment: the renewing birth of the goal ahead.

STAGES OF INITIATION; BEGINNINGS IN "FAUST" AND IN HEGEL

Neither man nor anything about him has yet savoured himself or itself. Still, it is generally asked how and whence one can enter into this being-for-itself. It is a question of knowing, of penetration, of self-encounter on all sides; and throughout recorded history this encounter has been represented as occurring in stages—at various levels. Every form of initiation through instruction happened step by step, even when the goal ahead was not in any way the self, but the sun or some other superior astral and mythical phenomenon, in which man is not to be found and in whose rays he even fades away. But there is no secret procedure of initiation (from that of the primitive puberty rites to that practiced in the caves of Mithras and in the Gnostic cults) which did not proceed in stages of increasing elevation—i.e. of consciousness.

Superstition prefigures the graduation of the path of knowledge, of its inferior and superior peaks or viewpoints. This is especially apparent in the practice of wearing different masks in order—while dancing, oath-taking and miming—to enter into the being they represented. Here, too, belong the various orders of "ravens," "eagles," and so on, in the Mithraic initiation ceremonies, and also the Gnostic division of men into "hylics," "psychics," and "pneumatics," together with the different levels of understanding in the exegesis of Scripture that correspond to these three categories.[17] Christianity removed this caste system, but not the hierarchical theory of apprehension within the knowing subject himself. Hence the mystic Hugo of St. Victor taught the following stages: the carnal eye (*oculus carnalis*), which affords sensuous and recollected perception; the eye of reason (*oculus rationis*), which offers access to the knowledge of perception; and the eye of meditation (*oculus meditationis*), which opens up the vision of God. Subsequently, the path of this contemplation itself was portrayed by Bonaventure in an aptly named work: *Itinerarium mentis ad Deum*—a veritable guide-book for the soul on its way to God. In it seven progressive stages of contemplation are developed with great meticulosity. But the clearest of such works was that on the stages of knowledge, the *Gradus ad Veritatem* of Nicholas of Cusa. The first step is the *sensus,* which provides the intuitions but also images that are still confused. The second is the *ratio,* which allows classification by number and, distinguishes between contraries. The third is the *intellectus,* which shows contraries together as being joined dialectically, and contiguous as dialectically sublated (the *coincidentia oppositorum,* or concordance of contraries); "What the understanding (*ratio*) separates, the reason (*intellectus*) joins together," says Nicholas in his *De conjecturis.* A fourth step is the *visio,* which should then reveal the full concordance of all contraries in an infinite unity. Therefore not only dialectics—the capacity of synthetic reasoning, as distinct from mere antithetical understanding, joins Nicholas of Cusa with Hegel, but still more the qualification that each higher stage, in the various forms of knowledge themselves as well, is the *praecisio* of the immediately preceding, lower one. In addition, Nicholas's three modes or classes of

45

knowledge (the fourth level, the *visio,* is intended ultimately as a stage not of conceptual knowledge, but—*sine comprehensione* —of intuition) offer an objective classification of three levels of (qualitative) existence, which they gradually disclose. The *sensus* corresponds to body, and potentiality in matter; the *ratio* to soul, the reality of the individual, the otherness (*alteritas*) of the world; and the *intellectus* to God, absolute necessity, unity (*unitas*). And the viewpoint and its objects are like the steps; the pyramid is again not unrelated to Hegel, as a pyramid of cognition and *cognoscenda*—both of knowledge and of things that are knowable. Hegel never refers to Nicholas of Cusa, although he was still (or once again) well known in Hegel's time (even a mediocre work like Tennemann's outline *History of Philosophy* of 1818 devotes an entire paragraph to "that ingenious Cardinal of Cusa"). Nevertheless, the *Phenomenology of Spirit,* which Hegel himself called his "voyages of discovery," is clearly indebted to Nicholas's teaching on the stages of knowledge—as if the whole *Itinerarium* had been included as part of the work from the start.

Here, in the entire systematization of Hegel's *Phenomenology,* we find the instructional equivalent to Goethe's *Faust.* According to its Preface, the *Phenomenology* was originally intended to present only an educative, and up-lifting form of instruction: as "the path of natural consciousness, striking towards true knowing." The more distant "seven-league boots of the concept" (as Hegel puts it elsewhere) correspond to the mythic magic cloak of Faust; and the progress of a methodical subject-object relationship has no less as its goal the moment of knowing oneself "in a good sense." In Hegel's educational manual, the goal—or "being-for-itself of the spirit"—is reached by six steps of sense-certainty, perception, self-consciousness, reason, spirit, and absolute knowledge. Each of these stages is again profusely sub-divided. And the whole process of instruction represents in the subject as in its object, growth—or the coming-to-be of knowledge—proceeding in oppositions from the merely im-mediate, still uneducated in-itself of its content, up immanent ladders, to the result (mediated with itself) of its content. From the initial sense-certainty or the mere now, here and this, the spirit is raised in the historical process to its configurations, or forms, until it is charged with no configuration other than one alien to it. Phenomenology is therefore the "representation of knowledge appearing," the "coming-to-be of science," and—from the pedagogical viewpoint—"the path of the soul, which travels through its successive configurations as stages marked out for it beforehand by its nature, so that it may refine itself to spirit; for it passes through full experience of itself until it reaches cognizance of that which it is in itself." But, because of the *world-view* that constantly offers itself in a new aspect on each new level, there is no resting in an experience which is merely pedagogical or concerns only the formation of the individual self. For the formation occurs just as much in an objective and organizational as in a subjective and educational sense; and with each new level of the subject there arises equally a new stage of the object, and conversely: "This new moment contains the nullity of the first; it is experience transmitted above it." Therefore, together with the forms of consciousness, the forms of the world occur as manifestations that are always more precisely manifest.

Looked at more closely, this is a mediation between the "I" and the "not-I," in order to advance them mutually. This mediation is amicable to the world, though of course in a certain sense it is also inimicable to it, inasmuch as no thing is taken and, as it were, retained as it is—statically. Dialectics is critical and will be bluffed by nothing; it is none other than the joint forward-movement of the Hegelian phenomenology and the ascent of the Faust itinerary. In each of these man counts as a question and the world as an answer; but the world also counts as a question and man as an answer. In each of them the subject wishes to experience that which is apportioned to all men; but the object also experiences the subject's self-recognition. In both these great works of exodus and homecoming, the subject does not merely observe, but conserves and preserves. In neither is man an ostensible shepherd of being. In both he is rather the *agens*—the same yet intensified *agens* that allows the configurations to proceed, transform themselves, and rise into realms (spheres!) that are ever more appropriate to us. Hence the decisive theme of *work* is added to the motif of travelling (and also learning and teaching) in the *Phenomenology*. It was Marx who first pointed this out. While Hegel proceeds through history as a subject-object relationship, and just as much as an object-subject relationship, this correlation becomes for him men's work on objects, and equally the *transformation* of objects for man. Or, as Marx puts it in the *Economic and Philosophic Manuscripts of 1844:* "The outstanding achievement of Hegel's *Phenomenology* and of its final outcome . . . (is) that Hegel conceives the self-creation of man as a process, conceives objectification as loss of the object, as alienation and as transcendence of this alienation; that he thus grasps the essence of labour and comprehends objective man—true, because real man—as the outcome of man's own labor."[18]

But in the *Phenomenology* even this work-relationship remains a relationship of the informing-informed experience of history, by means of which (as Marx says subsequently) the educator is himself educated, and his formation itself becomes transformation. Therefore, not only character but talent forms itself in the current of the world's stream; and on neither side is tranquillity indulgence.

A COURSE IN THE FACULTIES; THE WORLD IN STAGES

Man's peaceful learning has long been pictured as a process in which the appropriation of the material advances towards the light. If this means progress from the easy to the difficult, then of course an approach—an initially appropriate movement—is required in order to respond, and exploration comes before the material and genetic element of the matter. In exploration the wood is commonly seen before the trees, and the appearance before and more easily than what is basic to it. The initial bases of learning itself are as different from those of the matter, as the bases of knowledge from the real bases. The rising of mercury allows the rise of heat to be known—but the first does not bring about the second. The shadows on the moon might allow one to deduce the presence of mountains on the moon, but obviously the shadows have nothing at all to do with the origin of the mountains. Only when a great amount of knowledge has already been acquired can its progress and development and those of the matter itself come to the fore. Until then, therefore, the advance of appropriation, although it is and remains a process, does not yet occur in conformity with the *factual* genesis. The mediaeval educational system was not (or hardly) *objectively* divided into a *trivium and a quadrivium*. The *trivium* consisted of the disciplines of grammar, rhetoric and dialectics; the *quadrivium* of those of geometry, arithmetic, astronomy and music. In this system there were still vague traces of the old patristic idea that the pupil should proceed through arithmetic to the concept of size, and through music to that of harmony, in order then, by means of astronomy, to raise himself to the heavenly. With their "seven liberal arts" the *trivium* and *quadrivium* offered in the main a form, even a mirror, of the spirit learning, rather than of the world. On the other hand, the "encyclopaedias" of the time offer a quite different progression of both formal and factual knowledge. The *Speculum quadruplex* of Vincent of Beauvais already features something near to the distinctive breach between knowing and the world; it is divided into mirrors of theory (the form and matter of knowing), of history, of nature and of morals. This is obviously not a purely receptive-pedagogical progression, despite the tranquil and still undynamic methodology of learning. But in the great philosophical *Summae* of Albertus Magnus and Thomas Aquinas, in particular, this extra-mentally directed arrangement is decisively converted into a succession of levels with an objective real intention, even though the order of things is biblical-mythological and not the actual developmental-historical *ordo rerum*.

Thomas constructed his system of instruction in accordance with St. Paul's dictum: "Of God, and through him, and to him, are all things"; thus the Foreword to the *Summa philosophiae contra gentiles* indicates that what pertains to God in himself (ontology) should be examined first; then the emergence of the creature from him (cosmology); and finally the return of the same creature to God (soteriology). And despite a relative degree of demythologization, the progression of ontology - cosmology - soteriology (mediated through the influence of late-scholastic philosophy on Christian Wolff's system) is still clearly discernible in Hegel's in-itself, outside-itself, and for-itself of spirit. Of course there is a significant distinction, not only (as is obvious) with regard to the enlightened, merely conceptually mythological content, but with regard to our present concern: the relationship with the sequence of studies and the *Summa.* For in Hegel there is an end to (or at least an extensive mending of) the rift between the process of learning—especially of inquiry— and the appropriate method of the gathering matter itself. Even the stages of knowledge of Hugh of St. Victor and Nicholas of Cusa, which recur (*suo modo*) in Hegel's *Phenomenology of Spirit,* also make pedagogy the optics of occurrent objects, of the unfolding contents of things. The *Propaedeutics* which Hegel devised for the lessons he gave when Rector of the Nuremberg Gymnasium, includes, in the midst of a refreshingly accommodating course of philosophy for untrained schoolboy minds, the "firm advance of the thing that really matters." Not without reason, the classifications of the *Phenomenology* are repeated in small in the *Propaedeutics,* which itself advances by means of an interaction of pedagogy and material—of thought and being. Therefore a (not, of course, homogeneous) unity of motion, of travel, of process, occurs in both advances: both in the subject's journey of instruction and in the objectively "developed" material of the self-developing world. It is significant that this unity is present—and is most instructive for the pupil—when, above all, the development of *thought* no longer (as in objective idealism) omits the *matter* of development or, at best, leaves it inverted. Then the subsequently operative, undischarged force of a process of instruction as the world, of a process of the world as a *sequence of information*—is retained.

50

This arrangement proved significant. It offered the opportunity for rapid yet orderly glimpses into a kind of syllabus and timetable of things themselves. Now, as it were, the action of Schiller's poem took place in the shadow of the lecture-rooms, or rather in the over-all time-table that determined the sequence of the subjects treated, or their ascending order. And when this succession is not stabilized afresh (i.e. empirically, as in Herbert Spencer's world, fanning out as it ascends from the simple to the developed), instead of permitting hearing, seeing and thinking to subside before the audience in the various lecture-rooms, it allows them their first glimpse of encyclopaedic arrangement. The university is then a true microcosm, provided that the *universitas litterarum,* which can find its place here, is not reduced to a mere temporary roof over objectified specialization. Unfailingly its philosophical interest is closely related to the ever-stirring self-extraction process of the nexus of sciences, in spite of one-sided Philistines and remote subtilizers. Of course, it cannot be claimed that this interest was common (or even merely tolerated) in the universities of the nineteenth century and after. The light of philosophy burned far away from them— far from what Schopenhauer called the "professional philosophy of professors of philosophy." Yet that caustic genius begins his essay on "university philosophy" with this necessary judgment: "The teaching of philosophy in universities is of benefit to the subject in various ways, allowing it a public existence and the unfurling of its banner before the eyes of men; thus its existence is continually brought to mind and noted."

Ultimately, however, when it is noteworthy, this very existence of philosophy (even within the university—and there precisely) does not stop at the unity of the sciences—the one ship, the same ocean, the same direction in which they progress. Philosophy existed before the division of labor (which also brought about the separate categories of specialization), and it will exist after it—in a new society; just as it now represents the spirit of the *universitas literarum,* or at least is bound with all its force to proclaim that spirit. Precisely in this objective vocation, the correspondence of the system of the sciences (hence

51

also of its *universitas litterarum*) becomes equivalent to a world journey, to its total *changing panorama,* within the pursuit of study itself.

The self-impelling line of Schiller's poem, of *Faust,* and of the *Phenomenology* can be traced (now with reference to the university) in two significant judgments. One (the more institutional) is offered in Kant's *Conflict of the Faculties,* the other (with a veritable universal guide *in ordine studiorum*) in Schelling's *Lectures on the Method of Academic Study.* Consideration of both may illuminate *transparent* study with actual *studium generale* (even from the viewpoint of the university Faculties, the division of which into four can be traced back to the beginnings of the University of Paris). Kant describes the Faculty of Philosophy as the only one in which the book of the world will be read and understood without extra-scientific interference; whereas the so-called higher Faculties of medicine (still closest to philosophy with regard to freedom), jurisprudence and theology are tied to "sanitary regulations, common law, and the Bible." Nevertheless, in the common confines within which philosophy touched on the other higher faculties, by means of apparently intrinsically academic questions of demarcation, Kant also saw an opportunity to travel a considerable distance along the philosophically *material* aspect of medicine, jurisprudence and theology. Kant calls this an "elucidation" of the conflict of the Faculties; and such elucidations include formal *"expeditionary reports,"* wholly concerned with the scholastic problems of their motivation. Thus, at the boundary of philosophy and theology, there are questions of scriptural exegesis; at that of philosophy and law, the question whether mankind is constantly progressing towards a better life; and at that of philosophy and medicine, the thesis of the power of the human mind-and-heart to control by mere resolution its sick and morbid feelings. All this is a summary though not un-constitutive extension of academic boundaries, and probably only his advanced age prevented Kant from offering at this point a formal encyclopaedia of the confines between Faculties (as reflected spheres of experience).

52

What Kant omitted, Schelling took up in his *Lectures on the Method of Academic Study*. Above all, under the guise of advice, these lectures lead into and between the multiform sections of a world-view. The world-view of world-views itself is that of the sciences, in their problems and circumstances around 1833, elucidated by means of Schelling's current philosophy. The initial intention is pedagogic: "When a young man first enters the world of the sciences at the beginning of his academic studies, the more sensitivity and enthusiasm he has for the whole, the less he is able to obtain any impression of it other than that of a chaos in which he can distinguish nothing, or that of a great ocean on which he finds himself cast without either a compass or a star to guide him." The predominant intention is universalistic (therefore especially intelligible today), and opposed to anarchic specialization: "You know that a theory of the methodology of academic study could proceed only from the actual and true perception of the living connexion of all sciences; and that without this all instruction must needs be dead, soulless, one-sided, and even restricted. But it is possible that this requirement has never been more pressing than at the present time, when everything in science and art seems more forcefully to be striving towards unity; when even that which is apparently most remote touches on the sphere of unity; and when every vibration which occurs at its center or near it, is more quickly and, so to speak, more directly conveyed to its several parts." The last intention is ultimately the representation of mundane problems, so to speak in the inner line or in the outline of academic study itself, as arch-transparent study: "It is not possible to penetrate the particular divisions of academic study and to erect, as it were, their whole structure on first principles, without at the same time pursuing the ramifications of science itself and constructing it as an organic whole. . . . To a certain extent, this ground-plan could constitute a *general encyclopaedia of the sciences*." Accordingly, what might be termed "travel-pictures" now follow, and also the changing panoramas arising from the study of mathematics and philosophy, theology, history and law, physics, chemistry and medicine—all from the view-

53

point of knowledge, in which "subjectivity appears in objectivity." Thus study is paralleled in the subject-object relationship, with the world as "knowledge appearing."

A few years later, Hegel's *Phenomenology* made the comparison between *pedagogics* and *process-metaphysics* much more acutely and forcefully, although Schelling's mere suggestions keep close to the given academic situation (i.e. to its degrees and Faculties). He allows the lessons of the world-process to echo in the table of lessons—the syllabus; he joins the existing course of instruction (as it received and concerned the student) with that of the world, in a particularly pointed and instructive manner. There is more in this than mere considerations of didactic organization; from this basis Schelling could have illustrated his entire contemporary system of development—what Marx calls his "sincere youthful theories." If artificiality and especially some peevish quirks are removed, the method of comparing the sequence of studies and the objective sequence has the advantage that study (with all its ultimate demarcation problems) actually understudies the world process. To be methodical is to go the way of the thing itself, and the way of the thing itself demands *universitas*—a genetically articulated totality of outlook. And here is the *totum* itself (the whole that would actually be the truth): initially, very latent, in embryonic form, here in the real-and-utopian notion. This is the meaning of the travel-form of knowing, which has been handed down to us in so remarkable a way. It is a *non-static* meaning— *in the object of travel* as well as in the subject who travels the path of knowledge.

A CIRCULAR JOURNEY OUT

Back again to Hegel's syllabus—to the syllabus of a world spirit that educates itself in stages, dialectically *en route* from the in-itself, by way of the contrary apart-from-itself, towards the subjective in-and-for-itself—the starting-point; thus the gigantic tour of the world-spirit, consisting of nothing but circles winding back thetically—antithetically—synthetically, ends finally with the snake-ring of the world, as the "circle of circles" (this is true of the traveller too, if he does more than simply glance back). The final in-and-for-itself would be only the in-itself mediated with its contrary on a higher level. In other words: the initial thesis, as "pure being," as "abstract right," or as a merely "symbolic art-form," and so on, is not so much developed into a something new, as developed-out and reproduced at a higher stage. In spite of lively e-motion ("with every limb intoxicated"), in spite of a constantly starting process, the world for Hegel is "ready." Accordingly, there is no possibility that might not already be realized: "actuality is the unity of essence and appearance"; there is here no essence that has not appeared, that is not phenomenal. The interdict that could thus cause the process-journey and way of process to arch back again is easily recognizable in the *anamnesis* extending from Plato to Hegel: as that anti-journey in the journey itself, whereby (as Plato asserted in the *Meno* and the *Phaedrus*) all knowledge is only recollection or recovery of what has already been seen.

Being interpreted, the finger on the mouths of children in those Egyptian pictures belongs to the angel of pregnancy who has led the foetus for nine months through the worlds beyond. The child is born with a cry—as if of falling—and the angel seals its lips, for only in the course of its life will the child remember what it once saw; until the angel of childbirth reappears (though now as the angel of death) when the man has enclosed within himself all that he had forgotten but in his lifetime must remember, and thus come to know.

Plato inserted this very ancient myth in his teaching on *anamnesis*—the doctrine of the pure and simple return—with the implication that the soul can know and discover nothing new at all, apart from what it has seen in the eternal ideas as a travelling-companion of the gods before its birth. That which has been enjoys primacy over that which is to come; indeed, very being (or essence) itself is identical with having-been-ness. The origin occurs only as archaic *archē* (in Hegel, at least in his ontology, altogether "before the creation of the world"); and the dialectical cosmology of the disciplines is therefore only a journey-*anamnesis* to logic-ontology *ante rem*. Above all, Hegel's *Philosophy of Religion* and *Philosophy of History,* at the end of the system, *expressis verbis* are designed only to fill out with flesh and thus reproduce the skeletal categories of his pre-mundane *Logic.* Therefore, with Hegel, the *anamnesis* does have a place in the form of travel of his world spirit; contrary to any agreement, as a tribute from process to cycle. Nevertheless, the implications of Schiller's poem apply here, together with Faust's magic cloak and Hegel's seven-league boots of the notion; and apply precisely against any halos *ante rem.* The thesis of the in-itself, of the beginning, is so un-preoccupying that Hegel calls it "the poorest of determinations"; and the world-flow is now one whose content is supplied from the tributaries of its historical journey, and not from an *anamnesis* of being like to nothing at the beginning—a truly weak source.

Hegel's own temporal pathos remains sensible to the ring of Saturn in which it is inserted; the dialectic kicks against the circle—which means, yet again, that not only knowledge of the world but the world itself is on its way—with so many testing points, tendential configurations and process-figurations of a halt; therefore it is a journey which is wholly incomplete. It is wholly incomplete precisely in its essential being, for no appearance has yet become its essence, and each semblance is a self-experiment carried out for the first time. Ultimately, philosophy is regulated not by the kind of probing which peers below itself, but by the open outward journeying of the subject impelling its substance towards the substance which opens up its own subject; and, in all this, the longest line (the course of the world) is still the shortest path.

9. The Faust Theme of the "Phenomenology of Spirit"

I. Not all poets are Faustian (as is recognized). Nor all learned men (as is well-recognized); the pedantic character of Wagner in *Faust* would suit most of them better. Yet every thinker worthy of the name is close to the inquiring Faust himself; to the man at his desk through the watches of the night, looking for answers and the one needful thing. The appearance and image of Faust are taken from the thinker, as are his doubt and his grinding concern for certainty, for proven efficacy and potential, for improvement and instruction. Here nothing large is accomplished without suffering, without courage to venture upon unknown waters. A versatile and adventurous longing for experience *beyond* what is known and what has happened, and the testing spirit: these are Faustian. The rash yet elaborate efforts of the man trying limits are related to the Faustian will, and display the same characteristics of youth and age.

II. But it is another question whether the Faustian character has been diffused in accordance with its original. Of course there are the many variations on the figure of Dr. Faustus—the man who oversteps the limits in the old legend. He has had so extraordinarily compulsive an effect on the authors of the various adaptations, that, from the puppet-play to the most recent post-Goethean efforts, neither the monologue nor the magic cloak is missed out—i.e. the unimpeded journey into the magic far-off, the ever eerie depths. Nevertheless, only Goethe effectively maintains the Faust theme, the impelling motive of Faust —its power, breadth and depth. And only one work of philosophy (through persistent modulation of the theme of world-travel) offers a counterpart to Goethe's *Faust*—and that is Hegel's *Phenomenology of Spirit*.

Both have applied and elucidated the old legend material in similar ways. It is astonishing that this relationship of the two works should not have been noted frequently and adequately. It is not a matter of the yoking together of heterogeneous figures by means of an idea from a quite different source—as often happens in the case of works that differ essentially and chronologically. "Kant and Goethe" it was once; but "Hölderlin and Kierkegaard" is still one of the same private abstractions— contradictory and often repugnant comparisons that offer no more than a bridge between occult resemblances, and not ob-

jective connexions in the originals—as in the case of *Faust*
and the *Phenomenology,* where they eventually show themselves to be firm and impressive. They agree with one another
materially, both in their social basis, in the essential structure
of the work, and in the content which determines that structure.
The sequence of publication makes no difference (*Phenomenology,* 1807; *Faust* Part I, 1808; *Faust* Part II, 1832). For
even if Hegel did not know the puppet play (with so much of
Goethe's material *in nuce*)—which is unlikely—Goethe's early
version, the *Fragment,* had been available from 1790, and
therefore at an appropriate time for the discussion that was
then beginning between the "I" and the "not-I," between spontaneity and the world, and which was at the basis of the *Phenomenology.* Of course this *Fragment* did not include anything
as decisive as the wager on the moment of fulfillment, and still
did not reveal whether Faust would, as in the traditional legend
(unsympathetic to him), go to hell. But it did contain the statement which is almost a summary of the substance of the wager,
and which also appears as a résumé in *Faust,* Part I: "And so
what is allotted to all mankind/ I shall savour in my inward
self/ . . . And thus my self will widen and embrace the self of
all mankind." Although the continuation is rather surprising in
its reference to Faust and mankind—"And in the end I'll share
their doom—the shipwreck of mankind"—this catastrophic
note is taken from Dr. Faustus' journey to hell in the still un-
illuminated and obscurantist legend; taken because the *original,*
genuine Faust, a figure of the Renaissance, fell into his enemies'
hands—the hands of Protestant-obscurantist orthodoxy which
(together with its Luther) hated that "fool reason" and in
general every kind of creaturely impulse of power and spirit.
Hence, in the first Faust legend-book the Doctor had already
become the notorious magician; and, unlike the pious man of
God and simple believer of Wittenberg, this "Epicurean and
theorizer" might justly be carried off by the devil. It was Goethe
who first restored the original Renaissance dimension to the
character: without any "Faustus' screams," the terrorism of
"in aeternum damnatus est," or any interdiction against over-

stepping what until then had been the set limits for mankind. The "doomed" is there still only as an alien trace of the play's forerunner—for the magician does not travel "at a considered pace, from heaven, through the world, to hell." Consequently, Schelling, on reading the *Faust-fragment,* already prophesied Faust's salvation—on the grounds of the "over-all serenity of design in the first draft." And above all, closer to Hegel and the parallel movement of *Faust* and the *Phenomenology,* the social and historical impulsions from which Goethe wrote the *Urfaust* (in 1774–5, shortly after Hegel's birth)—the incentives of the revolutionary bourgeoisie—were still influential far into Hegel's youth. They were the same suasions which led Hegel to erect a May-pole, and which united him with the *citoyen* of Hölderlin's Greece, with its free *polis* and seemingly joyous Universal Nature.

Admittedly the *Phenomenology* itself no longer has anything in common with the Jacobin May-pole; and Thermidor had signalled the end of the French Revolution. But for that reason it was even closer to the later Goethean adjustment to the world, namely with the reciprocal I-object relationship, as that through which passed, experiencing the world, not the subject of the *Urfaust* (or of *The Sorrows of Werther, Götz von Berlichingen,* the *Ur-Tasso,* and the *Ur-Wilhelm Meister*), but that of the *Faust-fragment.*

III. Time, says Marx, is the space of history. By this, he means that it holds together the phenomena which occur within it, and gives them the same economico-social ground. For both *Faust* and the *Phenomenology* this was the awakening of the bourgeoisie that took place in Germany too. Both works have their origin in the consciousness of the bourgeois ego, of Rousseauian subjective emotion, of the enlightened "venture to know." Both works were written in the light of the dawn of German bourgeois society; both, therefore, are optimistic. The foundation of all this was the private economic method of the rising entrepreneur—a type which, in a backward Germany, was hardly in evidence at the time of the *Urfaust,* and only sporadically at the time of the *Phenomenology*. But this type was pre-formed wholly within the older, increasingly class-conscious German *Bürgertum;* and whatever it lacked in actuality—as compared with Britain and France—it obtained as a lyrical, dramatic and philosophical reflex from those countries. It was the kindling of a more lively ideological stimulation of the subjective self: first of all oppositionist and emancipatory, and then (with the non-appearance of revolution) abated and increasingly "conciliatory"—though not evanescent. It is true that Germany's insignificant economic development had ensured the exceeding mildness of the German Enlightenment which *preceded* the "Storm and Stress"[19] period in German literature; and, as the opposition from the much more vehement emotional play of the forces of creative genius developed, it became a subjective and ostensible *antithesis* to the national Enlightenment. That is, to the very movement of Enlightenment of which the *Sturm und Drang* itself was part, for it represented the emotional counterpart (mediated through Rousseau) to the vital concern of the Enlightenment. Hence the themes of the *Sturm und Drang* period (individual liberty, humanity, the struggle against "unnaturalness") were, so to speak, unaware of their oneness with the themes and contents of the contemporary bourgeois *ratio*. Only natural law, as a common concern of the Rousseauists and the odious rationalists, consciously united the German "*irratio*" of the time with the classical Enlightenment. But, even here, Rousseau's Nature—his emotional oppositionist Nature—seemed to have no point of contact with that posited by rational natural law (which was just as oppositionist), or with the mathematical and harmonic system of laws to be found in rational physics. But there was also an objective encumbrance of the relationship of the *Sturm und Drang* movement to its apparent opponents, to those of Corneille and Racine, Christian Wolff, and even Gottsched. It was the particularly ill-comprehended and offensive union of the German police-state of the time with the otherwise bourgeois-progressive regulative mode—bureaucratic rationalism. Nevertheless, in spite of everything, in spite of the tameness of the German Enlightenment and the distortions (i.e. the irrational behavior) of the *Sturm und Drang,* nothing could be plainer than the connexion of the fundamental *Sturm und Drang* theme—the Faust theme—with the original Enlightenment: with the release of the bourgeois individual and with "Reason and knowledge, man's highest power." At the same time, this brought about a conscious return to the Renaissance, in which civil emancipation began and the type of the Faust legend originated—the individual who calls to mind both Paracelsus and Kepler in wanting to "assume eagle's wings and explore the mysteries of heaven and of earth." Just as, on the other hand, subjective unrest—this "every moment's insufficiency"—fires Hegel's *Phenomenology,* and in contradistinction to all fulfilled mundane forms, pushes beyond the fulfilled to an ever new "history of the experience of consciousness in becoming."

Both works are connected by the thrust of the basic proposition of emancipation, *from the subject outwards;* they are also joined by the mediation of "conciliation" (as aforesaid—though now in a better sense, that of mundane compensation in the style of Wilhelm Meister) *towards the object.* The intention was not only to approach and accept, but to e-ducate—objective maturity. And not escape was intended (a trace of petulant though feeble escapism), but precisely being-there in the flow of the world. For Goethe and Hegel themselves this object-world was, around 1800, no longer that of the worst form of *ancien régime;* instead, Weimar was the background to the restlessness of the *Urfaust;* and Thermidor and the founding of the Confederation of the Rhine to the *aporias* (or theoretical dilemmas) of I and not-I from which the *Phenomenology* first arose. So that the subject was schooled in the world, and precisely in the composed world of law and order. Pacified and reassuring in a reactionary sense as well—in that of the German *Misere,*[20] which is not missing from Goethe or Hegel, with a cynical and resigned conformism vis-à-vis even a world-course in which not the subject but the object had to sow its wild oats. Nevertheless, the central concern cast its light beyond the sphere of politics; truth would arise to extend the self not only to hu-

61

manity, but to the sphere of the world, to the rotation of the world itself, where it would always prove a dispenser of good, and thus be instructive. Faust, like Wilhelm Meister, is intensive—but in a quite different way; nevertheless a certain element from that novel about man's education entered into his continual striving. And the subject of the *Phenomenology* is from the start a Faust-like "self," for it extends itself to the cosmos (when writing the *Phenomenology*, Hegel produced an appropriately cosmological image in his description of Napoleon as "the world-soul . . . on horse-back").

Therefore the objective spheres in and through which the phenomenological subject educates itself have all the greater a reciprocal effect on it. The general and the particular, thought and the world, the consciousness and the object, should not be separated and oppose one another inimically. And objective self-education occurs and proves itself in the general *vita activa,* which is restless activity for the self of Faust, and increasingly potent labor for the subject of the *Phenomenology;* it moves through many different levels, mediating them with man at work, and mediating man with the objects worked. In this way Hegel surmounted subjective idealism, and won through to a kind of spiritually appropriate though objectively nourished realism, wholly in tune with Goethean objectivity and attachment to the world. Certainly in *Faust* as in the *Phenomenology* the initial element reappears, "no longer clouded," at the mediated end; in one work in a mythical heaven to which it has ascended through further activity; in the other in a mystical aether of the self-knowing spirit. In both works, at any rate, the "higher spheres" are external, and succeed one another in accordance with the activity of the journey out, the progression of the scenes, and the world's shaping. The Faustian element is always present in the *Phenomenology,* and the phenomenological element in *Faust;* the action is reciprocal by virtue of the common world movement from within to without that is as full of mysteries as it offers solutions to them. Therefore it can be said (using in the one case a Goethean, and in the other a Hegelian term) that Faust's monologue is the "ur-phenomenon" of the *Phenomenology,* whereas the substance, which is also conscious of being the mediating subject, is the *absolutum* of *Faust.*

IV. Both works are in continually renewed movement throughout. In Goethe as in Hegel this constant change of location is insufficiency—desire that has not been and must be assuaged. With the magic cloak and the seven-league boots of the notion, this lack is related to a type of longing and desire too old to have been invented.

The predecessors of the journeying self of *Faust* are probably well-known: the actual historical figure, the miracle-worker Georg Faust, was a vulgar imitation of Paracelsus. The magician of the Faust fable comprised elements of Simon Magus from the Acts of the Apostles, recollections of the scholastic philosopher Albertus Magnus (suspected of magic practices) and Paracelsus. Simon Magus belonged to a legendary tradition that went back, in particular, to Gnosticism and the (itself legendary) wisdom of Egypt. Frenzy was the punishment accorded the oriental hubris-figure who opened the chest of sacred mysteries and raised the veil of Isis in Saïs. Faust's rebellion in search of knowledge and his subsequent journey to hell are undeniably related to this taboo, handed on by Plutarch and Schiller; as to its most ancient source (also passed on in a hostile tradition through the priestly codex of the Bible)—the plucking of forbidden fruit from the *tree of knowledge.* In the case of Goethe, Dante's paradisal journey provided a model for Faust's journey in the here and now—of course with a secularized adaptation of the setting, apart from the final scenes in heaven. But instead of the Dantean *visio beatifica* at the end, there is the new form of Protestant striving, the *vita activa;* the new-style Protestant-bourgeois *Commedia humana* replaces the *Commedia divina* of a fixed and feudal estate; and there is an actively changing, ever newly unfolding world substituted for a preordained movement and setting.

Nevertheless, the Dantean spatial hierarchy affects Faust's world-spheres, and the changing panorama with its propounded then abandoned, ascending series of scenes. Conversely, the protagonist in Dante's poem also changes wholly as phenomena are observed and experienced; purifying himself (as Faust so often does) of the horror he has met with; drinking, in order to sustain himself for the ascent, from the streams of Lethe and Eunoe—oblivion and recollection. This subject is wholly conversant with renewal (with the *incipit vita nova* of each higher circle), and knows how the structure of each stage (whether as the history of appearance of the subject-object, or as an already determined hierarchy from above) must contain superimposition in succession, and succession in superimposition. Even in the mediaeval *ordo sempiternus verum,* the stage reached as a step forward is an *ordo temporalis* which tells the stepper-forward what o'clock—what *time*—it is in eternity.

When we move to Hegel's work, neither the element of journeying, nor that of a sequence of stages, is missing. Of course the laboring subject of the *Phenomenology* differs from the protagonist of *Faust* in having no miracle-worker at its birth, but rather the same, more recent *homo faber* from whom there emerged on the one hand the insatiable *Faust,* and on the other the consciousness that is constantly ready to begin. Extreme curiosity assists at this man's cradle; curiosity related not only to probing but still more to journeying—to the ship with wind-taut sails passing through the Pillars of Hercules on the title-page of Bacon's *Novum Organum.* The more immediate forerunner in Hegel's case is Kant's *spontaneity* of consciousness, transcendental generation out of the pure development of thought; in Hegel, however, there is the quite forceful, Promethean-idealistic claim that not merely the forms but the contents of knowledge, of the content of the world itself, are developed from it. And in addition the Creator of the world is also resolved into the productive subject; the origin of the world is accomplished in the stages of consciousness of it, of work on it. Therefore the journeying and ever recommencing element of the *Phenomenology* moves through a world in which there is no substance and where no substance is valid that does not travel with the producing subject and is not penetrated by that subject.

Eritis sicut Deus—"You will be like God," Mephisto writes in the student's book; and whenever at quite different periods in his philosophical works Hegel has occasion to mention the serpent in connexion only with the myth of the Fall, he defends him—as Lucifer, as another Prometheus, as the bringer of light.

In Hegel's system the serpent and the tree of knowledge first made man in helping him to consciousness of labor and to the labor of consciousness; without that man would have stayed in the "garden of animals"—and remained an animal himself. The connexions with the bourgeois "Titanism" of the *Sturm und Drang* movement (which later still reappeared in Byron) are unmistakable; in Hegel, production advances beneath the crust of that which has become, moving against it, undermining it. Even the now conservative Hegel uses the subversive image of the "digger-mole of the spirit" in the sense of that dialectics of production which Alexander Herzen later called "the algebra of revolution." This is the extension of *homo faber* in the subject of the *Phenomenology,* as the urgency of Faust capable *sui generis* of setting out on the great journey of the spirit—into the spirit as the most materially replete journey of all. Of course, it is a journey of which the subjective factor is allegedly only a spectator, and whose subject (according to Hegel's idealism) does not stay with man as the maker of his own history, but dissolves itself into a hypostatized world-spirit—a demi-urge. Nevertheless, this spirit is in no way the God who strikes from without, or the transcendent God, or the "beyond" of *homo faber*. Nevertheless, this world-spirit cannot help proving itself wholly as the Faustian earth-spirit, indeed as the exclusive spirit of history. For this very reason, instead of being the lifeless solitary, the immovable absolute, it travels, like Faust, through stages. And again has available to it not only a vast antecedent history with large stretches in common with the lay-out of *Faust,* but one that—much more than the plan of *Faust*—manifests a reprise of traditional and feudal forms of ideology in the midst of bourgeois-dynamic forms.

Therefore, like *Faust,* the *Phenomenology* is not—*mutatis mutandis*—unrelated to the ascending pattern of the *Divina*

65

Commedia. More so, for, led by a more accomplished Virgil, the reader passes through the Golgothas of defunct spirits, and see the categorial moments of the absolute idea graduated into the conscious, social and occupational configurations of world history. In addition there is another traditional predecessor, or prototypical essence, that is only implicit in Goethe's *Faust,* but in the *Phenomenology* explicitly determines the entire methodic *terraced scheme.* It is this structure—of the stages and steps themselves—corresponding to a subject not only of activity and labor but of ascent in an ascending self that has its own levels and is itself mountainous. This Dantean, virtually cathedral-like space, together with its different corresponding subjective-positions, has a particularly hierarchical reprise in the *Phenomenology,* in the midst of its dynamics, and increasing it. For, more clearly than the plan of *Faust,* in arranging its subjective levels (in accordance with the objective phenomena that are visible at this stage, and entangled with the subject), the *Phenomenology* takes up again very remote traditions of ascent—in this case from well before *homo faber* and his activity.

The division of the *Phenomenology* into "consciousness, self-consciousness, reason," into "spirit," and then into "religion and absolute knowledge," follows—with renewed emphasis—very old *mystical sequences of meditation,* or, to use once more the expression coined by one of these meditators (Richard of St. Victor in the twelfth century), a *Mentis itinerarium ad Deum*—a manual of the soul journeying towards God as the "object" of the final union, as the goal of every adequation of the spirit to the thing (that matters), to its own thing. Even in the case of Richard of St. Victor, the stages were called carnal *"cogitatio,"* inner *"meditatio"* and spiritual *"contemplatio"*; so that the carnal eye would see the material world, the rational eye that which was properly within, and the contemplative eye the spiritual world: *per simile simile percipiens*—perceiving like through like. In a still more Hegelian pattern, Nicholas of Cusa graduated the sequence of *"sensus," "ratio," "intellectus," "visio"*: so that "sense" offers only a clouded perception of things; the "understanding"—in accordance with the principle

66

of contradiction—discriminates between contraries; the "reason" sees contraries as compatible with one another; and "vision" sees them as coinciding in unending unity (the *coincidentia oppositorum,* or "concordance of contraries"). This *gradus ad Parnassum* has related examples that extend to the psychology of the Enlightenment. Indeed its even older forebears are clearly present in *mythology;* hence even magical agents are to be found among the sources of the *Phenomenology*—the seven-league boots, of course (as if for the initiation of a *mystes* of ancient times), but not the magic cloak.

But the stages to the history of appearance of spirit, from which the profoundest of all manuals of enlightenment arose, exhibit a remarkable and instructive parallel of a still mythological and then demythologized kind. In the Gnostic "initiations" the initiates removed the subjective clothing that did not correspond to the specific "imagination," simultaneously putting off the old Adam and putting on the new god of mastery in order to possess its particular essence. This was virtually the same procedure as in the primitive ecstasies of the masked dancers for whom the lion, bull or serpent mask put them in contact with the particular daemon thus portrayed. Idealistic (or, rather, not wholly idealistic) thoughts can for their own part remain in a singularly mythological if not pre-logical garb; thus increasing wariness of the doctrine of stages associated with cognition theory, but also awareness of its astonishingly fresh old age. Because it is an almost pre-historical phenomenon, it is not merely restricted to the static society of fixed estates, and with it the pedagogical-methodic change of levels does not come to an end. With Nicholas of Cusa there is of course no longer any trace of such frenzied superstition; and in Hegel there is no recollection of Nicholas of Cusa and his sensory stages. Nevertheless the *Phenomenology* realizes these different ways of perception with unusual precision, and even allows history (which is to be penetrated and experienced) to repeat itself three times (with three different emphases) on the in each case new level of appropriation of generic experiences: as a mere sequence of human *skills* on the levels of "consciousness, self-consciousness and reason"; as actual *history,* i.e. as the product of acts of human *generation,* on the level of "spirit"; as *conceptualized* history, i.e. as a history of the *renunciations, or alienations and counter-alienations of the self,* on the level of "absolute knowledge." And this very method of ascending stages, with an essence encountered in increasingly sublime manifestations, ultimately also illuminates (not surprisingly) the ascending self in the plan of *Faust,* and its expanding nature.

The arrangement of ascending stages that is present in both works (implicit in the one, explicit in the other), here and there —in *Faust* too—allows events to reproduce and produce themselves as new events at a higher level. The "reproduction" (even though it is a more sublime transformation) of the tragedy of Gretchen of *Faust I* in the Helena tragedy of *Faust II,* and just as much the "reprise" of the first meeting with Gretchen in Gretchen's second, heavenly prayer of distress that is converted so affectingly into gratitude for bliss—in *Faust* too all these spirals stem from a related hierarchy of stages like that through which the *Phenomenology* travels in thought. And one in which, according to the definition of Nicholas of Cusa, the lower stage discovers its "precision" in the higher stage—which, in this case, means the most precisely assimilated, more exactly expressed form of its mediated content.

V. Both works are particularly clearly related in their *dialectical* motion. The journeying of their "heroes" (in the one case Faust, in the other consciousness) and their presence in the "unrolling of happening" must occur immanently through opposition and contradictions. Since Faust's journey is, in the *Phenomenology,* a journey of dissatisfaction or insufficiency, it is directed towards completion and justice; therefore it must contradict everything in objective phenomena which in the long run does not satisfy it. The act of being present in events exhibits this journey as one filled with contradictions and sudden change, with a kind of objective Mephistopheles—i.e. replete with objective negation. Consequently, this no longer cynical but objective Mephistopheles identifies itself as the power which "always willing evil still engenders good,"[21] and also as an element of the world judgment (i.e. the Day of Judgment) in world history itself; of a total judgment, of course, inasmuch as it considers everything that arises to be worth abrogation.

Committed dialectical reversal appears in the words: "Reason becomes non-sense, and kindness vexation." Although Goethe otherwise frequently opined that the terminology of Hegelian dialectics was too bizarre, in a letter to Niebuhr he called the word *Zustand* ("state," or "condition"), with its connotation of immobility, a "wretched" term—since nothing stays exactly as it is, everything being changeable. And in his reported conversations with Chancellor Müller, there is the following description of the dialectics of *Faust* which lays particular emphasis on the new, on the production of synthesis out of negation: "There is nothing that is gone that one should wish to have back again. There is only an eternally new formed from the extended elements of what is now gone. Genuine longing must be always productive, striving to effect something new and better." Instead of "synthesis," Goethe also used the term *Steigerung* ("intensification," or "enhancement"); and—though under the influence of Schelling—he called the two basic forces of nature "polarity and intensification."

Polarity, according to Goethe, permeates all existence: in the formation of colors as the polarity of light and darkness; in the growth of plants as the alteration of contraction and expansion. *Intensification* occurs in and through polarity, moving towards the forward workings of harmony: "The final product of the constant self-development of nature is the perfected human being." Of course, these concordant harmonies do not themselves entirely accord with Faustian insufficiency, or with striving and tension towards Faust's heaven. Goethe is also still within the older kind of relative scheme that extended as far as Schelling: the *coincidentia oppositorum* which consonantly (too consonantly) relaxes the tension between its basic contradictions, so that negation is not itself preserved in unity to continue within unity its work of provocation. Nevertheless, the impulsion of Faust is implicitly and explicitly forward-moving and dialectical; it is that which is forceful and unsatisfied; that which satisfies every situation, but which no situation is already in a "condition" to satisfy. Consequently, *Faust* achieves the unity of striving concern and striven-for content even less readily and completely than do the end of the *Phenomenòlogy* and its moment of *having attained* to something in "absolute self-conscious spirit."

Hegel extended immeasurably his scientific treatment of the movement in *Faust;* extended it as immeasurably rich in contradictions, as forward-driving and provocative of movement forwards through all personal dissatisfactions and constantly crisis-laden situations. The contradiction of "life" and "dead objectivity" had already affected the thought of the young Hegel during his Frankfurt period—but still as unmediated contradiction, and in such a way that objectivity would even more clearly be death. However, the unmediated antimony of "life" and ostensibly "dead objectivity" extended itself as Hegel's mature dialectics struck through about the antimony in the impelled and therefore living *object itself*. Mephistopheles, the spirit that always negates, now enters fully into the real process, and must take effect and stimulate through negation; so that negation both contains the acid of scepticism and first allows "life" to beat as the pulse of the mundane forms that are subject to and in need of change. Or, rather, subjective contradiction slackens, and the subject of the *Phenomenology* is almost of necessity thrown out of its now inadequate objectivity, and into new spheres of adequacy; the impetus of objective contradiction (of "inconsistency" in objects) increases correspondingly and realistically. Contradiction no longer appears essentially as the determination of the subject, as in the *Sturm und Drang* movement, and in the monologue of weary satiety and flight in *Faust;* but also not as subjective deception placing itself objectively in the peace of reconciliation (if not with society, then at least in and with nature). Instead, contradiction becomes simultaneously an object-determination, related to Goethe's "polarity" and, above

70

all, to his "development"—the most important and hopeful objective determination in the world.

Contradiction, as Hegel's *Logic* says and as the *Phenomenology* already indicates, is "the root of all movement and vitality; only insofar as something contains a contradiction, does it move, and feature drive and activity." Wherefore the unity of the equation in no way ends in harmony between the contraries, but the "unity of unity and contraries"; or, as Hegel had already said before the *Phenomenology* was written, "the union of union and non-union." This guarantees difference *usque ad finem*—the prompting essence of dissonance, the thorn or spur reproduced in every determination on the way, and producing itself at each new level.

This is an essential distinction between Hegel's dialectics and all previous candidates; it is not stilled in the unity of contraries or contradictions. Therefore it comprehends the world as a history of dissonance instead of a temple of harmony; it attributes the primacy of peace to mysticism and not to the historical and real world. This tenacious contradiction is also found in the wholly objective Mephistopheles, so that Hegel can say (mythologically) that God does not dwell in the sphere of difference (of negativity). Of course there is a point in Hegel's *Aesthetics* where the philosopher of the negative, with a curious sideglance at Goethe's *Faust,* rejects the representation of negation as such. This change could have a religious basis—because of the so-called absence of God in difference. Nevertheless, it is still strange when the same Hegel who, from the *Phenomenology* up to and including all his other works, distinguished "the seriousness, the suffering, patience and labor of the negative" from all "vapid edification," now disavows the "mere negative." This is the conspicuously anti-Mephistophelian passage: "The reality of the negative can correspond to the negative and its essence and nature. However, if the inner notion and purpose is already futile in itself, then still less will the already inward ugliness admit a genuine beauty in its external reality. By particular adroitness, strength and energy of character, the sophistry of suffering can try to introduce positive aspects into the negative; yet the only impression we receive is that of a whited sepulchre. For in itself the mere negative is insipid and exhausted, and is either void or repels us, whether used as the suasion for an action, or merely employed to contrive someone else's reactions. . . . The devil by himself is a bad, aesthetically unserviceable figure, for he is nothing but falsehood in himself, and therefore a highly prosaic individual."

The passage is particularly striking when the following thoroughly sensible and realistic proposition of Hegel's is set against it: "People think they affirm something impressive when they say that man is good; much more impressive, however, is the statement that man is evil." Or when from among Hegel's many tributes to negation one selects only the following, quoted with particular emphasis by Lenin: "Indeed, if precedence were in question, and both determinations were to be maintained as separate, then contradiction would have to be taken as the more profound and substantial of the two." Nevertheless, "contradiction"—as presented in the rejection of Goethe's devil and of the celebration of negation elsewhere in Hegel—resolves itself by the distinction between the "mere negative" of the "negative in itself" and that objective negative in which precisely "the inward notion and purpose" is not "already futile in itself." And the whole fruitfulness of the "labor of the negative" consists— in *Faust* as in the *Phenomenology*—in that labor which is necessary to understand and to use the negative as effect and stimulation, as with Mephistopheles. Otherwise Faust as well designates the "mere negative" mythologically as the "cold fist of the devil,"[22] and Hegel correspondingly as the impression of a "whited sepulchre." In *Faust* and in the *Phenomenology,* not only dialectics but *active realistic problems* of dialectics are uniformly immanent, at least as a horizon.

VI. One does not forget something one has made an effort for, for the sake of which one has been extended. *Faust* and the *Phenomenology* are, with a consistency equalled by few other works, bent upon a *goal* from the start. The reference in *Faust* is the wager, together with the content of the "Stay!" addressed to the fair and arrested moment. This means in part that Faust —the active agent—never allows a relaxed "Stay!" to be addressed to any moment. The implication is that he will never be content to lie at his ease; and this intention is foremost in the acceptance of the wager. But as the play progresses, and definitely at its end, a second intention proves to be predominant— even the only essential one: that which would have the moment be a fulfilling and fulfilled moment, and therefore one that "stays" only if replete with substance. To use a scholastic term, this moment is the *nunc stans:* the "now" which has come to rest but is also fully open to its content. With Goethe this "now" can already be indicated in a moment of time that lifts itself out of concern and flux, insofar as this moment itself is resplendent with meaningful content. Situations of this kind are not transient—mere transitional stages in the movement of the epic or dramatic process—but, even though their passing is not to be arrested, display a characteristically lingering sufficiency, or (as Goethe himself says of the encounter with Helena) a "solidified" quality. Faust's entry into Gretchen's room; the sunrise at the beginning of *Faust II;* the meeting with Helena in Sparta and the temple, "in the moonlight so strangely close": as they unroll, these and other scenes seem somehow to be "framed" and to stand for an emphatically fulfilling *nunc stans.* However, this is clear only at the end, "upon free soil with free people," and therefore *at the moment* when Faust addresses *the moment* thus constituted with his "Stay!"—or, rather, feels he may now say it to the "presentiment" of exalted bliss. Unrest believes itself to be stilled in the notion, and by means of what is opposite to the "bed of ease" of inaction—action with *social content.* Whatever the extent to which this activity (a final idealization of bourgeois society deriving from the *citoyen* spirit of the French Revolution) does not still the unrest but is rather the continuing striving and exertion of the "immortal" Faustian element,[23] with Faust's avowal (that allows him both to lose and win the wager) an arc is unmistakably described, leading back to the theme of the initial movement—to Faust's

73

wager with Mephistopheles, and to the Lord's wager with Mephistopheles.

Hegel stresses the fact that a start can be made at any point on the circle of knowledge. But the *Phenomenology* is directed also to the preservation of an *omega-motive* formed early on. In this case it is the motive of "immediacy," which as such moves through alienations and appearing forms towards "mediated immediacy." This is joined with the reward promised in the Preface to the *Phenomenology* and awarded at the end— the "transformation of substance into subject." Even if, in the Preface, the *Phenomenology* lets everything amount to and depend on "apprehending and expressing that which is true not as substance but just as much as subject," the conclusion asserts the arrival of that which everything depends on and amounts to: the substance, in its having become that which is for itself, the absolutely self-conscious subject.

After its initial "immediate self" has run through the spatial sequence of natural forms and the temporal sequence of historical forms, the *Phenomenology* presents itself as "notionalized history," having paced out Faust's "circle of creation" up to the mediated being-for-itself of the initial immediacy of being-this-one, of being-this in itself. Therefore, out of the first empty and hence restless certainty of a mere being-this-one, being-this in itself, comes the movement of the spirit in which it consciously unites itself with its content: "To urge forth *from itself* the movement, the form of its knowledge, is the work that it completes as actual history." When the substance of the ascent is again aroused in this way, it returns—by way of the preservation of all its alienations and the reciprocal alienations of all these alienations (recollection)—to its subject's absolutely self-mediated immediacy. The *Phenomenology* as a whole reveals itself (in the aforesaid sequence of subject-object-subject) as "that movement of the self that disposes of itself to itself, immerses itself in its substance, and as a subject has emerged from its substance and entered into itself"—up to that mediated fulfilment of the self with its content, that in the end "sublates the difference of objectivity and content." Whereupon the *sub-*

ject is no longer endowed with the object as if it were alien to it; and therefore the universal Faust of the *Phenomenology* lands in the Ithaca of his proper homeland—in the pure *nunc-stans* sphere of being-for-itself. Unfortunately, this means that the self of the *Phenomenology* is not merely no longer endowed with an alien object, but no longer endowed with any object at all; and this in spite of Hegel's declared world-intent, his (in common with Goethe) reference to the objective, and his concrete pleasure in externality. With Goethe the latter joy did not leave off in the realm of the moment of fulfillment; to the end Faust remains just as fully an external character as when, during his life, he sought and supposed in the world what Goethe calls the "answering counterparts" to his inward self. He made his way into the world, like the subject of the *Phenomenology;* but, more materially, for Faust *objectivity remains also in the being-for-itself of the moment of fulfilment*—and in this precisely as a just objectivity. And it remains not only to the Faustian self of the concrete action, but to the Faust who is essentially and constantly intent upon knowing, who is instructing and receiving instruction in the heavenly setting. Even the transcendent sphere that is still so lofty remains a sphere, and therefore a circumference; and is filled not only with a vis-à-vis of human beings (even though they have passed on), but just as much with Nature (even though it is transfigured).

Objectivity, however symbolic it may be, remains the objectivity of within-without: here on the transcendent peaks, on which anchorites who have left the world are encamped[24]— which indeed they utter and which they themselves are; there in the outspread canopy of heaven in which the Madonna displays her mystery. Even in this highly spiritual location, objectivity-nature does not cease; it remains, even though in an extremely mythized form and always as parable (*Gleichnis*), maintained and raised up as if on native soil. Not, therefore, as no object, but (as intended) precisely as one with which the subject is no longer burdened as if with something alien—but without disappearing as an object (in this case as Nature transfigured). Of course this is immersed in the being-for-itself of

75

that other *chorus mysticus* at the end of the *Phenomenology;* the exit into the entry posited solely as spirit consequently leaves no room for the objective-filling—unless it be that of surmounting-preserving recollection. But still, in the *chorus mysticus* of the conclusion of the *Phenomenology* as well, there resounds the anticipated moment of fulfilment which is unmistakably related to that at the end of *Faust;* and it resounds by virtue of the fullness that without objectivity is never maintained and awarded. "Everything transient is but a parable"; and, regarding the being-for-itself of the content of the world: "From the cup of this kingdom of spirits its eternity foams up to it";[25] between these epiphanies not only substance reveals itself as subject, but a "blue, outspreading canopy of heaven" displays its mystery. Hegel's object-revocation for the sake of mediated, fulfilled immediacy, just as much implies the taking-up of the object, so that its absolute spirit may not be "a solitary entity deprived of life."

VII. *Man* as question; the *world* as answer: This Goethean and Hegelian movement and reference outwards is just as much a constantly renewed start from the basis of man—from the striving self-concern of Faust, and from Hegel's liveliness of the self. Both prevent the mere acceptance of a given existence; both display Goethe's "worldly answering counterparts," just as much as Hegel's "reward of a frequently intricate route and as frequent exertion and concern." This form of prevalence of the subject over the particular environing society and over Nature establishes true genetic methodology. It establishes Faust's journey through the world as one of which the world itself perceives something. It establishes the experiential history of consciousness in the *Phenomenology* as just as much one of the object-world that man fashions and manipulates. Not last, it establishes the truth of active-historical materialism, as distinct from the merely intuitive-natural scientific materialism of the eighteenth century.

Man as question; the *world* as answer: In the concretely impelled subject-object relationships of Goethe and Hegel this means equally: the *world* as question; *man* as answer; that is, man who has come into his own (self) together with a necessity and nature mediated, grasped and humanized with him. The *Faust* motif of the *Phenomenology* is therefore, seen from this starting and finishing-point, the *Phenomenology* motif of *Faust:* the history of the production of man and his world through movement and labor. In *Faust* and the *Phenomenology* the subject-object is in the same way that of humanity ascending in contradictory self-liberation out of alienations and through them. Even though this process was seen as if through the medium of the still progressive bourgeois society of the time, *Faust* and the *Phenomenology* stand with us at a new threshold —the threshold of a socialist society. The inscription above it reads thus: *"The end of the object with the liberated subject; the end of the subject with the un-alienated object."* A more than merely postulated inscription in the both restricted and immeasurably large world of alienation. Growing self-alienation, the conversion of all men and things into commodities, the new bureaucratization of existence through officialdom and objectified industry: these are just as much signs of the condition of being "burdened with something seemingly alien," as of our objectification that is still so inadequately identified. Nevertheless, by the same token, this very alienation could not even be observed, let alone condemned, as that which deprives men of liberty and the world of soul, if there were no measure for its contrary—i.e. that possible becoming-itself and being-with-itself by which alienation can be judged. This being-with-itself is certainly nowhere adequately present as yet; and empirical facts themselves are for the most part only the empirical facts of reification. Yet the being-with-itself that has not yet been attained lives all the more intensively in real anticipation; thus it is in the subject as *intention* pointing ahead, and in the correlations of objects as the still on-going *process*. It is process (other than in the case of empirically concluded facts) that as it goes on its way is replete with artefacts, testimonies, experimental forms, works of art, songs of consolation, and even promises that clearly point farther ahead. It is also full of frag-

77

ments, looking forward to the attainment of being-in-and-for-itself, yet with its utopian star in the blood. "This steering forward to a star, a joy and a truth in the face of empiricism . . . is the only way by which truth can still be found; our questioning about ourselves is the unique problem, the resultant of all world-problems; and the framing of this problem of self-and-us in everything—the opening up of the gates of return home, a movement that swings through the world—is the ultimate basic question of utopian philosophy" (*The Spirit of Utopia,* 1923). It is clear that this no longer coincides with a primacy of recollection over hope, of what-which-has-been over that-which-is-to-come, or even with essential being as being-that-has-been. But it is clear too how the consistent theme in Goethe and Hegel of travel and impulsion to travel is maintained through so many stages of an Odyssey-world that could also be an anticipatory, truly homewards-bound world.

10. Models on the Way, and Hegel's Thesis

". . . *the model concept could also mean that the world of so-called facts is itself still in a thetic, model state in itself.*"

When a man is about to make a journey somewhere for the first time, he has nothing (as yet) to relate about it. But he does have a more or less regulative idea of what lies before him. Even when it does not fail to hit the mark, it will be for the most part too general; yet this kind of prefiguring, with not too great an exertion of the imagination, is both usual and useful. Of course it can happen that a too rosy preconception is not effaced when the destination is reached. Yet the dim sketchy image is corrected and the false conception disappears if the traveller is observant and versatile. But the more substantial image will remain somewhat wistfully behind what is actually seen, or continue undisturbed alongside it. Therefore, even in recollection there are two "sights worth seeing": that which has become visible, and which in this case is often disappointing (although that can weigh down only an unobjective spectator), and that which was foreglimpsed (in this case often delineated only from the depths of the heart). In science, of course, one is far removed from such eventualities; in this case preparation is *ab ovo* a more solid undertaking. Nevertheless, here too, as aforesaid, there is a self-adjustment of the factual circumstances that are to be experienced, before they are approached experimentally or even hermeneutically. Here there is a thorough heuristic computation beforehand, even indeed (with certain features in common with the preview of a journey) a kind of heuristic *imago*. One has only to think of Schliemann's preliminary, orientating, almost credulous idea of Troy, and similar phenomena all the way to Goethe's much more sober yet just as conceptually pictorial *prévoir pour voir* (even, indeed, *pour comprendre*) before he discovered the intermaxillary bone in man. The gods ordained the sweat of labor before the granting of the prize, but Minerva[26] plainly required only an initial trust, a thesis of acceptance, of prefiguration. A *thesis?* But didn't Hegel himself describe this initial member of his dialectical method as "estimation"? Not as heuristic computation; but certainly as a still abstract universal of "beginning," which is the first version of the particular? And, further still, in the country travelled in itself, not in the mere entry to it, does not any thesis postulated—pre-postulated (inasmuch as, with Hegel, everything merely methodological is pre-lucidated *in reality* —not proceed as an approach in the *world* also? Indeed, Hegel puts a thesis before each of his dialectical world groups: i.e. logically, as "being like unto nothing"; legally, as still "formal legal correlation"; aesthetically and historically, as not yet unveiled "initial symbolic art"; and so on. Reason enough, so it would appear, to confront a very different kind of preliminary computative thought—indeed preliminary computative being— with the non-lament of *Faust,* i.e. with the pre-statements and pro-positions in the Hegelian version.

For Hegel especially it was wrong to talk of all assertion in advance, even from the basis of the mere "I." Of course, Hegel would understand this more as irresolute, biased *opinion.* In addition the "recesses of the heart" are in question here, for they contain too much emotion, a "soft element for which anything it fancies is imaginable." For Hegel, instead of referring to this kind of "opinion" (which he considered to be almost wholly distasteful), it was more respectable to speak of a religious trust, in the sense, too, of an inner experience. This is "belief" or "faith," defined as a "category of direct knowledge" (certainly only "direct" in the sense of "im-mediate" and not "mediated" knowledge): "Belief is a form of knowing, but by 'knowing' one usually means a mediated, cognitive knowledge." Every certainty of faith is therefore distinguished from "truth," although—for the Christian Hegel—specific religious trust should have the same content as philosophy. For this very reason, however, it should aim at *philosophic development;* it has, says Hegel, a tendency in that direction; and its very devotion, "which comes from thinking and that which is thought," must, for this very reason, in order to be true, proceed to reflected knowledge of its content. Its divine content, which before that is only the sentiment ("the warm hazy fulfillment," the "formless whirl," of devotion) reflects on itself, towards its conceptualization, towards the truth of its notion. Hegel makes a profound comment on this no longer non-mediable, but reflected and verified devotion: "In it I am only as reflexion at the same time from God into myself." Here, as we see, even *a priori* trust, as faith with content, is already categorized by Hegel wholly as a thoughtful indication of a "concrete notion of the thing" (itself). But still with considerable "recesses of the heart," for which reason is able to posit only guardedly a kind of pre-figuration and thesis-definition of a content that in faith is still unmediated. But what of the *thesis itself* in its dialectical, and above all dialectical-objective initial role and initial postulatory function? For Hegel, that which is thesis, together with its postulate, is properly only that which is non-mediable, still abstract and general—the undeveloped in-itself of its concern. Therefore every dialectical world-group commences with this kind of skeleton-map before the concrete development of content, and only then do the particulars concretely mediated with

80

the particular follow—the mundane transformations of what was previously only abstract and general. They explode dialectically by virtue of the contradictions expressed in this pre-universal; when the antithesis—this "turning-point," this "negative-rational"—has occurred, they return in the developed, only now concrete universal of the "positive-rational" synthesis. For Hegel this remains the initial stage of taking possession of the world in thesis form, that is therefore also undertaken beyond the voyages of discovery of his *Phenomenology,* which is itself an *anticipation* of his "real philosophy."

Can the thesis therefore (to use a significantly estranging anachronism) be explained by means of an *objective model-indication?* It cannot, if the antecedent element of the thesis is conceived not as experimenting and probing, but only as undeveloped. Equally it cannot be explained thus if further progress itself loosens the rigidity of the thesis but at the same time only fills the outline of the thesis with what was already within. A thesis is only capable of being an *experimental* model where the result is not already prepared in the thesis itself—even as a mere silhouette. Nothing in such a thesis can be explained as a "model," least of all when the thesis-like element in the world is relaxed, precisely where its pre-figuration appears in an actually postulatory and not simply heuristic-empirical form. The latter is above all the case in Hegel's *Philosophy of Right,* whose thesis should contain only given formal law, and not by any means the norm-establishing model and draft of a "true law" as was available in the natural law. Natural law—precisely the form that does not accord with law as it exists, is so little treated here by Hegel as an objective draft-thesis, that he allows himself to consider it only as phantasy in the sense of his "recesses of the heart." Indeed, the model in the English, American and French revolutions is transformed from a (previously phantastic-moral) construction "into a trivial abstraction above the real and practical essence—Right." The same should be valid for all model-thinking that offers moral postulates; for, says Hegel, just as little as logic is able to give an answer to the question of what truth is, would one be able to seek out a code of ethics "in this absolute practical reason, since its essential nature consists in having no content." Even though Hegel offers here an immeasurably justified criticism of the formalism of Kantian ethical postulates, there is little justification in a philosophical draft or outline (the designation of Kant's essay on peace)—therefore thought in outline—being deemed without content, only because this content, of necessity, is not already concretized but exists only in a normative model-state.

Nevertheless, in conclusion: Hegel's *category of thesis* as such has itself an outline *ante rem,* i.e. *in processu* in itself—that outline which tries to understand how to make out that which fills and fulfills with content. *In terms of method every heuristic model is a thesis; and every thesis with concrete anticipation indicates a concrete experimental model in the form and forms of the world itself.* There are two indications of this in Hegel which are particularly illuminating, even though Hegel would not have distinguished them as "theses." But Hegel's dialectics was a *heuristic* model of the first order "in a still idealistic guise" (which had to be discarded). And an *anticipatory* model of the first order is available in the quotation from Hegel about the "reflexion from God into myself," as the most profound model-indication of an anthropological critique of religion for the purpose of an eventual legacy from religion in the unknown *humanum.* This suggestion of the "model" comes in an unexpected place: in spite of what in Hegel was concluded from the first, in spite of the anamnesis in Hegel—that wishes to learn nothing new in the process; in spite of its merely returning circuit, as an ostensible "symbol of rationality." What has been called the "experimental thought" of explanation is available in a different form—with the true irony of positivistic fate— even in great philosophy, in the most metaphysical of philosophies, and precisely in these. That is: with as little positivism as possible, conveying scepticism about thought, as the vehicle of progressive conceptualization, from mere thinking into the thesis of its *objective matter itself.*

82

This kind of experimentation, this order of model-semblance, is properly present not only where a philosophical journey is intended, but where the *process-course* of the world is to be clarified in its own objective *test-forms* and *thesis-experiments* —often rounded off, but always open because utopian.

INDICATIONS
OF UTOPIAN CONTENT

11. Overtaking

To go along with something can be cowardly, as when a fellow-traveller trims his sails to suit the wind of fashion—doing what's done because he thinks it's rather smart. Then it doesn't really matter whether he agrees with the particular way things are going, or whether he's even aware of its implications. A stylish reefer-jacket doesn't make a sailor a proficient helmsman: style doesn't have to be *understood*. Yet people don't go along with the really swinging thing just because it's fashionable, but because they hope to get something out of it. That sort of implication is readily understood and fully accepted; the profiteer really keeps abreast. He falls behind only when the going doesn't seem so good—for him. But your smug bourgeois can't change the pace of things by himself. He's always against everything he's not used to.

Different is the lot of those who have stayed motionless and feeble, out of step with the present like weak pupils who don't keep up even though they'd like to. This sort of existence can approach the bourgeois condition; but it will stay unprovoked, shut up in itself, as long as the antiquated situation doesn't get too bad. In among these types you often find some who are not just behind the present but who remain stunted, can't get ahead, because they're inherently weak. Next to these workaday "contemporaneous" types are those who are not (or not merely) retarded, but just have to be called *non-contemporaneous*. Among them are all who are remote from the course of the present—in some out-of-the-way spot or small town. They're petty-bourgeois, and provincial into the bargain—for theirs is a way of life much older than that of people who just aren't keeping up. Some of them in particular (fishermen—and among peasants not merely the foresters) lead an existence and use working methods strongly reminiscent of earlier times. Although modern appliances, newspapers, the radio and so on have undoubtedly had a gradually refining effect and to a certain extent given things a contemporary finish, there are still types from other centuries among us, in spite of the modernizing process. The extreme superficiality of modernization in certain cases was shown by the adherence to the Nazis of precisely these social groups: the blood and soil ideology seemed to accord seductively with the ancestral call for discipline and morals. Of course the former exploiters of this kind of retrograde tendency—the *masterful* men of the moment—are themselves quite untouched by it. Not that they really see through and into the impulses of their time: they are just wide-awake in seizing the opportunities it offers. This isn't a case of being non-contemporaneous, yet it doesn't mean they are consciously overtaking the times, or being *ultra-contemporaneous*.

This last doesn't mean going along with things. This ultra is wholly contemporaneous, but he doesn't always relish the way of his world. He shows genuine resistance to a dominant evil of his time, and genuine acceptance of what is intermittently meaningful in it. Both qualities grow on the same tree of the tomorrow in today. Accordingly, in order to assist the birth of tomorrow, his thinking is deeply concerned with matters of present moment; in order to guide them, and overtake the moment. Overtaking does not merely presuppose the discontented—individuals who are dissatisfied by the pace and state of things. And it does not presuppose only desire and expectation, and the capacity to dream ahead. Of course that is necessary in order not to take things as they are, by resigning oneself to them instead of revolting against them and rejecting them when necessity demands. But overtaking must not be an abstract affair: either in the form of a putsch or insurrection that turns out to be mere aimless tearing ahead, or in the shape of an illusion of good fortune hereafter which no one actually has the slightest idea how to get to. That is enthusiasm or fanaticism —only ostensibly in the vanguard, even though it looks as if it has a pretty impressive lead. A fanatic doesn't really overtake; he just over-estimates. To avoid this, of course, it's still necessary to go along with things—not of course with things as they are, but with things as they go: as they could really and possibly go, in their positive direction and tendency. If you're overtaking, you can't ignore the way things are going; in fact, to keep your eye on the road is the most important thing. Or to put it another way: if he's not himself in the stream of traffic and aware of its pattern of flow, the anticipator can easily arrive at a destination quite different from the one intended. And later in the course of history circumstances which are over-estimated show absolutely no trace of the overtaker who overtook too fast. Still, the last advice for your average Philistine (who sticks fast by going along) is "hasten slowly." For *ultimately* it is necessary to *overshoot* the mark in order to reach it.

12. The Meaning of Utopia

Dreams come in the day as well as at night. And both kinds of dreaming are motivated by wishes they seek to fulfill. But day-dreams differ from night-dreams; for the day-dreaming "I" persists throughout, consciously, privately, envisaging the circumstances and images of a desired, better life. The content of the day-dream is not, like that of the night-dream, a journey back into repressed experiences and their associations. It is concerned with an as far as possible unrestricted journey forward, so that instead of reconstituting that which is no longer conscious, the images of that which is not yet can be phantasied into life and into the world.

Castles built in the air of walks or quiet moments are often empty and shaky because the fixtures and foundations have received little attention during construction, yet often extravagantly daring and beautiful because building-costs were never a consideration. A child's dreaming about presents belongs here; or a youth's desire to be a great man—and above all the image he has of his future beloved. Azure day-dreams range from everyday conceits of self-assertion and revenge, from commonplace reveries of gold linings and gold brocade, all the way to plans for world improvement that are no longer merely focussed on the deserving ego of the dreamer-anticipator. All the same a sort of rhapsodic enthusiasm can carry the dreamer over any consideration of means and situation; equally it can keep him restless and expectant, full of life and therefore of possible striving ahead.

This is especially true if the day-dream emerges from its mere make-believe. Still, its make-believe pursues it in its actual form, and indeed has a social function in doing so. All those distracting, gilded con-dreams belong here: all those sham images that misrepresent u as x; all those daytime dreams of pulp literature in which an impossible stroke of good fortune befalls some poor devil, and in which the happy ending is unhappy deceit. The day-dream of good fortune operates quite differently in the oldest known form of utopian narrative—the fairy tale, where there is no mere distraction and voyeuristic palliation, but a vital stimulus and direct relevance. The brave little tailor conquers the ogres with cunning, that Chaplinesque weapon of the poor, and wins the beautiful princess. And plenty without labor as a frontier-motif is alive in the tale of Cockaigne, where the mountains are changed into cheese, sausages hang from the vines, and the streams are flowing with best Muscatel.

The geographical utopias are not so remote from Cockaigne: the land of milk and honey is the best-known, the earthly paradise that Columbus imagined must lie to the West has been most fraught with consequence. But fairy tales also contain imaginative forecasts of some technical-utopian objects—by no means only in a magical and hence impossible form. "Table, lay yourself!"; the magic horse; the magic carpet; Aladdin's admittedly absurd wish-fulfillment properties; all offer their services and evoke longing: "If only man could do that!"

One might even cull fairy tales to make an inventory of discoveries that have not yet been made—a kind of technical utopia. Bacon's *New Atlantis* already offers an array of this type. Yes, social, geographical and technical utopias are available in the fairy-tale world, and the utopian quality is found in many more areas than its restriction to the so-called utopian romance or novel would allow. This limitation of the utopian theme must eventually cease, yet its somewhat tepid extension to "science fiction" is hardly even half-adequate. Instead, from the consciousness of children and young people (not only desirous or covetous of new things, but believing themselves to be virtually bubbling with new ideas); from times of social and cultural upheaval; from the products of the creative spirit and the countries that it has really appear above the horizon for the first time —lands that were never thus seen before, have never thus been before: from all these there arises a utopian territory of problems, categories and spheres that itself was hardly ever thus envisaged. It is not only that there is (or need be) no tallying with mere humbug in day-dreaming, or with "fairy tales" in the pejorative sense, but that even the social utopias themselves (though admittedly they form the main stream of all utopian books) function only in the midst of other, specific utopian areas, with reference to human culture as a whole—indeed to Nature independent of men.

Accordingly, life as a whole is full of utopian projections, mirrored ideals, dream-manufactories, and travel pictures. In literature there are the characters who stride out ahead into what is not yet manifest; from the wretched Zendelwald in Keller's *Seven Legends,* or Michael Hellriegel in Gerhart Hauptmann's *And Pippa Dances,* right up to the incomparably powerful *Don Giovanni* and *Faust*—not forgetting the admonitory figure of Don Quixote. Above all, for particular spheres of endeavour, there are the utopian lands of medical, technical, architectural and geographical expansion and attainment. Even in the ancestral territory of utopias, the social utopias are not alone: next to the images of possible human happiness in the social utopias, the rational images of possible human dignity are projected as teachings of natural law. And closer still, in effective existence, regarding not perspectives but perplexities, there appear the (always overtaking) moral guiding images and ideals, and the topically still unidentified no-where whither music leads. And again, think of the particular utopia in the many images conjured up as specifics against death, and closely related thereto, in the wish-mysteries of various religions and the Christian mysteries of hope. Item: *humanism has developed in utopia,* and philosophy is justifiably speculative since the actions, testimonies, problems and postulates of not-yet-being mark out its central and in no way merely empirical area of operation.

However, it is necessary that precisely the more common dreams should set their sights appropriately ahead. Their outlines have abandoned mere private wishful thinking, and in most cases have nothing at all in common with it. Nevertheless a distinction has to be made between the utopistic and the utopian; the one approaches circumstances only immediately and abstractly, in order to improve them in a purely cerebral fashion, whereas the other has always brought along the constructional equipment of externality. Of course only utopism, as it reaches out abstractly *above* reality, need not fight shy of a mere empiricism that undertakes only another form of abstract apprehension *below* reality. A real utopian critique can only proceed from a viewpoint that is adequate, that does not—so to speak—correct or even replace over-flying by a factistic creeping.

"That's rather utopian!" as a smart depreciative judgment from businessmen's lips, a kind of stock dismissive remark, has at any rate become a phrase denoting anxiety about the future in general. Nevertheless, and precisely because of this, an essential and fundamental distinction must be made between utopias that come to be in the abstract and in the concrete. Social utopias in particular were liable to be abstract, because their designs were not mediated with the existing social tendency and possibility; indeed, they *had to be* abstract, because (precisely on account of existing tendencies and stages of development) they came too early. Hence the Utopians all too frequently had to construct the outlines of a brave new world out of their own hearts and heads—or, as Engels says: "For the basic plan of their new edifice they could only appeal to reason, just because they could not as yet appeal to contemporary history."[27]

This is true even of the (by no means inimical to the world) schemes of Owen and Fourier (federalistically oriented), of Saint-Simon (with a centralistic orientation); it is properly true of the real and very different "anti-world" humanism in most social utopias. At all events, even if utopian humanism did not accord at all with the existing world, then it may be said: the worse for that still existing world, and the more inevitable and fruitful thought about justice. For this reason, Engels (independently of later deviationists who were far from having a scrupulous concern for humanism) also remarked of Owen, Fourier and Saint-Simon: "We delight in the inspired ideas and germs of ideas which everywhere emerge through their covering of phantasy." Both in Fourier's "critique of existing social conditions" and in Saint-Simon's "breadth of vision of a genius, thanks to which almost all the ideas of the later socialists which are not strictly economic can be found in embryo."

And so, lest the undeniable abstractness of this social-utopian element be exaggerated, the clearly social *schedule* of all these schemes for world-improvement must be remembered. In spite of excessive dreams of the future, they are touched by their own time—precisely because their connexion with it is always negative. Because, unlike ideologies, they do not vindicate and proclaim the ruling class of their society, but rather wish to lay the plans for the future dwelling-place of a new class making its way through for the first time; and do this half as—so to speak —advance billet parties, and half as effective architects of *homo homini homo.* Hence the great Utopians spoke out on behalf of the *coming* bearers of society, and for the particular *tendency to come.* Obviously the interest they assume is no existing, ruling one, but one on the ascent. With Sir Thomas More it is a freer market system, with Campanella the period of absolutist manufacture, and with Saint-Simon the new, more socialized, magical *"de l'industrie."* Consequently, even the utopia that was still an abstract outline (not to mention that which had reached a concrete form) was not the cloud-cuckoo-land implied in the use of "utopia" as a pejorative term by those who found it absurd or even abhorrent.

But the main thing persists and, persisting, holds more importance than the journey's plan, which is not decisive in principle. The main thing is that utopian conscience-and-knowledge, through the pain it suffers in facts, grows wise, yet does not grow to full wisdom. It is *rectified*—but never *refuted* by the mere power of that which, at any particular time, *is.* On the contrary it confutes and judges the existent if it is failing, and failing inhumanly; indeed, first and foremost it provides the *standard* to measure such facticity precisely as departure from the Right; and above all to measure it immanently: that is, by ideas which have resounded and informed from time immemorial before such a departure, and which are still displayed and proposed in the face of it.

With the prefigured utopia of the *citoyen,* Hölderlin's *Hyperion*[28] rectified the bourgeois (then established); and the *citoyen* was not shelved but remained particularly and naggingly insistent. Of course there is Schiller's dictum with its idealism, its resignation: "Only that which has never come to pass never grows old." But when applied to the *utopicum* and what that postulates, its truth relies solely upon a utopian interpolation— the adverbial "not yet." Then, *cum grano salis* (seasoned with the salt of historically exact understanding, the understanding of latency), the saying is just: "Only that which has never yet come to pass never grows old." Is just in respect of that life beyond labor hinted at in almost all social utopias; or in respect of a coming to be human through fit aims and profound perspectives about us. This not-yet was imaged and imagined in the obviously utopian constructions of great art and religion; it remains unsatisfied in the before-us. Indeed, the more an age sceptically renounces or is dogmatically removed from the not-yet, the more it solicits it. But in any case, without the dimension of the future, conceivable for us as an adequate future, no empirical being will endure long. And so in ages of growing darkness at least a *horror vacui,* and in ages of increasing enlightenment always a *plus ultra,* shows that utopian consciousness is alive.

All the worse then, if a society that will no longer be reconciled in an abstract-utopian manner, but demands the way to the thing itself, errs on the way—and errs dangerously. All the worse if the revolutionary capacity is not there to execute ideals which have been represented abstractly, rather than to discredit or even destroy with catastrophic means ideals which have not appeared in the concrete. Action will release available transitional tendencies into active freedom only if the utopian goal is clearly visible, unadulterated and unrenounced. Even though the utopias have at best promised their still so palpable optima, but have promised them as *objectively* and *really* possible.

13. Utopia in Archetypes and Works of Art

It was proper that dreaming ahead should image that which lay ahead. Only later was a concept added; for a long time it did not seem an essential part of the concerns of Thomas More and similar imaginists. Of course this is only apparently the case, and indeed a fundamental misunderstanding of such works; nevertheless these utopian constructions were cast in a flawlessly narrative form. They might even be called fairy tales of the commonwealth, not mere "novels" of civil society. For this fairy-tale element had a more than fictive reference, and did more than equate dreams with shadows. Many fairy tales, such as those about poor children or brave young men, are powered by a distinct image of happiness, and are already on the utopian march towards the happy end. Similarly the fairy tale of the commonwealth was reminiscent above all of the ancient folk dreams, which had their own already utopian characteristic in the shape of a search for "good fortune."

But the fairy tale, replete with phantasy, also has a utopian connexion with so-called "pre-logical" forms—a figurative connexion, yet one in no way antithetical to the conceptual form of a later period and its enlightenment (which indeed is itself an image). The fairy tale is related to the acquired or "inherited" *basic images* of the imagination—the famous "archetypes." Whereas the fairy-tale element, as distinct from the saga, is not a degenerate form of myth but has a quite specific origin that is even inimical to the stratified higher social form of the myth, the archetypal figurative material largely remained in, and expressed itself by virtue of the context of myth. Consequently the archetypal was stressed not only as pre-logical but—in essence quite unjustly—as wholly irrational. Jung, for instance, relegated the archetypal to an unthinking "unconscious of more than 500 thousand years ago," from which he would allow it only to "emerge"—quite without future—as no more than *regressio*.

Yet archetypal images have constantly recurred in history (just think of the dancing on the ruins of the Bastille); and, in the midst of their mythical context, the really ancient ones often display a wholly luminous, thrustingly utopian sense and purpose—for example, the radiant memory of the Golden Age, conceived of as a buried age, or as one approaching in the future. The latter sort of archetype is already intrinsically utopian and also appears in the fairy tale as the archetype of Cockaigne or the Never-never Land.

Many other encapsulated archetypes—such as the invisible castle, or the saviour king, and their mythized context—must be cracked on their so to say utopian content. Admittedly a very few archetypes of suppression and lordship—such as the Medusa, or even the Olympian god and his lightning—are without hope. But the encysted or openly humane archetypes are not devoid of the utopian notion; they do not brood, diluvian and mysterious, in the depths of the unconscious. Everyone knows them from his present existence—by the power of images which strike, stimulate, and illumine. Everyone meets them in works of art and in the situations and forms of conflict and resolution they feature; in the inexhaustible power of unequivocal symbols; and even in multi-ambiguous allegories. The enemy, the mother, the saviour; the tyrant's castle and its taking by storm; the labyrinth and Ariadne's thread; the dragon killer; and the saviour in the form of a servant, and his disclosures (Odysseus arriving home, or Jesus): these are archetypes. All scenes of *anagnorisis,* of sudden recognition, are archetypal (Electra and Orestes, Joseph and his brothers), as is the way out of darkness into light—the Exodus from Egypt towards the land of Canaan. The latter fundamental image is already *archetypal utopia* itself; to which land belong the clarion-call of the Gallic cock,[29] the storming of the Bastille, and the dancing on its ruins, when Perseus whose second name is Revolution has liberated more than Andromeda. But it also appears in archetypes with a much more tenuous reference to the Golden Age and the obstacles in its way; for without their crypto-utopian dream enclaves they would all be one gigantic sport or Olympian phantasm—or just the player's Hecuba.

The dream of the conformably human has no faint heart: it looks out for *more.* Not only in the basic acquired images, but in additional newly-fashioned images—in the *works of art* that apply them. Therefore a "significant" work does not perish with the passing of time: it belongs only ideologically, not creatively, to the age in which it is socially rooted. The permanence and greatness of major works of art consist precisely in their operation through a fulness of pre-semblance and of realms of utopian significance. These reside, so to speak, in the windows of such works; and always in windows which open in the direction of ultimate anticipation: driving forward, soaring, or achieving towards a goal—which is never a mere land in the clouds above. One of the most obvious examples of this kind of work of art is *Fidelio,* informed with the striving of the French Revolution.

But even *static* works of art of enduring quality are not

wholly circumscribed by their transient existential basis and its corresponding ideology. The slave-holding society of the ancient Greeks, for instance, is a social form we can hardly conceive of at the present time; yet the art of that very society has provided a "model" by which, much later in time, a form of art has sought to prove its value, or to show its contrasting power. Mediaeval art was tied to a feudal, hierarchical society; today its feudal-clerical patrons can be evoked only as phantoms in comparison with their reality; yet the inwardness, order and mysticism of the art of the Middle Ages still affect us, for they rank above the hierarchies of their own time, and above the mythological out-there. In these cases a "cultural surplus" is clearly effective: something that moves above and beyond the ideology of a particular age. Only this "plus" persists through the ages, once the social basis and ideology of an epoch have decayed; and remains as the substrate that will bear fruit and be a heritage for other times. This substrate is essentially utopian, and the only notion that accords with it is the utopian-concrete concept. Art is not merely the ideology of a particular ruling class, let alone its propagandist servant. And a combined application of sound economic analysis (which removes scales from the eyes) and of sociologistic-schematic blinkers (which serve only as replacements for the scales), even in the form of Georg Lukács's theory of literature, merely obscures the utopian perspective of every great work of art.

Even in the midst of the most triumphant feeling of achievement, there flashed and shone that so often so intractable blue, the fleeting promise of that which is missing: the supreme illumination and above all the most human thing that the perfection of a work of art can afford. Hence Michelangelo called Ghiberti's bronze gates for the baptistry in Florence, "fit to be the gates of Paradise." Of course this ecstatic declaration says nothing of Paradise itself; yet its initial promise of a threshold (Yet that thy *bronze* gates of heaven may ope, and give sweet passage . . .) must be counted with the blue and gold in the window as a further utopian characteristic of a great work of art

95

(indeed, of a great work *tout court*), and as the least deceptive of such signs.

Utopian consciousness remains wholly without deception inasmuch as the moment of its fulfillment is still outstanding—and certainly not for sceptical or agnostic reasons. Yet this utopian consciousness in a work (of art) does not obscure its binding goal with solutions, let alone with mere reified *means* from the route to that goal, and then (even on a Hegelian level) offer an absolutized half-light in conclusion. Its reason for not doing this is superlatively *real*—the most objective correlative ground that utopian consciousness possesses: The world-substance, mundane matter itself, is not yet finished and complete, but persists in a utopian-open state, i.e. a state in which its self-identity is not yet manifest.

If things are commonly seen only as they are, it is not uncommonly paradoxical to put at least as much trust in *their ability to be other than they are*. Therefore Oscar Wilde's remark about a map of the world without the land of Utopia not being worth a glance evokes no shock but the shock of recognition. True, things themselves offer only a dotted line of extension to something like that land; but all the world's positivists could not erase it from what really is so. Consequently not only the specific existent, but all given existence and being itself, has utopian margins which surround actuality with *real and objective possibility*. Consequently every work which represents and informs this possibility (and every work would accord with the *per definitionem* of "significance") is full of augmented horizon problems; and its own level depends on the level of such problems. Therefore great works of art can dispense least of all with the creative touch of poetic anticipation—not the concealment or repression but the pre-semblance of what, objectively, is still latent in the world.

This enables us to distinguish the *hermeneutics* of archetypes from that proper to works of art. All non-fairy-tale, non-aurora archetypes have to be opened up in order to discern their utopian content; but in great works of art (even in those that are obviously static and conformist), the self-light of this

96

utopian presence glows on the horizon. In a work of art, sorrow and anguish never remain *unillumined*—just as they are; and joy always dawns as a fore-glow, with the depth and emphasis afforded by shadow. Even the great tragic fall, despite all its blood, death and darkness, and despite the Cross, never has the last word in the work of art, which is ultimately still open. Hence the phenomenon of optimistic tragedy, with a faint though definite richness and fullness even when the end seems so black. Lukács rightly counters "pessimistic tragedy" with this assertion: "The greatest tragedies that we have inherited from the past do not show forth the inescapable vanity and necessary annihilation of human endeavours, but on the contrary the actual or actually recurrent struggle between old and new, in which the collapse of the old, or the fall of the new when opposing the old with weak forces, crowns the realization—or at least the perspective of the realization—of a higher stage of development." Admittedly Lukács's standpoint is again mainly sociological, and he is using the phenomenon of tragedy and its perspective only as a device for non-aesthetic comprehension of social processes; nevertheless, the surplus containing the perspective, and therefore the utopia anticipated here as well by the work of art, is particularly clear in the apparent paradox of optimistic tragedy.

Both depressive and revivifying works of art allow their characters and situations to decline or to develop to that limit or horizon of being where, somehow, after all, there are gates. Schiller's *Ode to Joy* shines beyond what has been experienced hitherto, because (although—and since—it is only an ode) it already names and summons perfect joy. Schiller supplemented this invocation of joy (it extends from "Daughter of Elysium" in a somewhat Kantian-postulative mode to the by no means factual though wholly utopian statement about the Deity: "He must dwell above the stars") with another in his poem *Columbus,* which is not concerned with Elysium but does say something about its attainable coastline in the utopian connotations of these verses:

On, keep on! Steer by faith,
And follow the reticent waters West,
Where the coast of the land as yet unseen
Must rise from this ocean.
Genius and Nature are ever joined,
And his promise will be her action.

Of course these lines are full of abstract idealism, but they also contain strength of purpose—will; and contain it (*qua* genius) in express conjunction with Nature which creates and naturizes. More than ever duty's call is to do what is within and not to abandon what lies without—not to leave it as it is; more than ever, that is, for every phenomenology of the "spirit" and of its works that makes no peace with the world as already given. Instead, the phenomenology of change and the changeable travels through the world in order to trace and advance what is not yet present in the world.

Utopia in works of art certainly makes fragmentary and negative the offerings of those that are significant, inasmuch as the world really signified in them is itself the least ready and finished of all: it is as often thwarted as it is seldom realized, as often traversed as it is seldom peopled. But an ode to joy is a most valiant effort, for it affords a venturesome even if—unfortunately—only a poetic premium; yet, philosophically too, no mean education is to be obtained from the testing end, and (more permanently) from the experimental beginning.

14. Scientific Imagination and Cognition of Facts; Process Knowledge

In terms of method every heuristic model is a thesis; and every thesis with concrete anticipation indicates a concrete model in the form and forms of the world itself.

98

NEUTRAL SUPPOSITION

Before what is thought is thought, what ought to be thought is opined. Not only because one is aiming at it and bent upon it, but because one's thinking *to* it grows from an initial thinking *of* it thought to oneself. Of course this preliminary, explanatory communion with self is already a thinking out *thus* to oneself, but about *the thus* nothing as yet is asserted.

Admittedly the *opinion* thus constituted is already directed to an outline, present in the mind, of how a case is to be conceived and therefore coherently grasped. But a thinking-to-oneself extended in this way does not yet claim to be true or false. Therefore every mere (though merely initial) opinion in this way still remains neutral, as yet commits itself definitively to nothing. Consequently the opining of such opinion extends from mere non-committal blether all the way to the cautious supposition that something is probably as it was thought to be, as thinking sketched its lines. And should the non-committal hot air become affirmative, it shows as prejudice—above all if it is general and conventional opinion. Or it appears—when just pulled out of the air—as a fast spieler's con-talk; and, on a more elevated level, as scientific and scholarly confidence trickery.

But all the banality and brazen impudence round about genuine, responsibly directed opinion cannot cheapen the good fortune that suppositions are possible. And suppositions do not stop at mere thinking in such a way, like that, if their supposing turns to positing such or such a thing like that. Although deception may often cling to the coat-tails of first suppositions, it is not their child. Indeed, without probing and testing supposition there would be no approach to scientific understanding itself; there would be imitators, but no more initiators. Before making an appearance rigor tests its strength, and tests it in play—in preluding.

SUPPOSITION—NO LONGER NEUTRAL

With increasing seriousness, therefore, mere musing becomes explaining: thinking it over becomes making it out. In this process the circles described by supposition grow ever narrower, and sensitivity to truth and falsehood grows ever finer. Calculation emerges from that merely neutral form which Meinong was the first to examine (though as pure vacuous form) in his book *Assumption.*

But the supposition whose content is *related* to—is approaching—the matter to be investigated, is no longer an empty form: precisely because it is in-formed by the in no way abstract material for the sake of which scientific suppositions exist at all and are themselves *differentiated.* They now face truth and falsehood without neutrality; for the initial amazement and questioning (which, as we have seen, are always at the basis of any such approach) become a no longer so immediately profound access to the given aporias—the impassabilities of the world. Hence, in supposition, the *objectively oriented* questioning attains to an immense mass of data that would otherwise be too immense to survey; but it is a questioning that has not only direction but calculation—regulating calculation that knows what in particular is sought after, and where approximately the illuminating response might be in the data amassed.

There are often alternatives in directed questioning born of mature supposition; and they are sometimes limiting though never illimitable. For example: Did Rudolf Hess fly to England in 1941 on his own initiative, or did Hitler send him? —Do bacilli always cause a disease, or can they also be mere concomitant phenomena? —Is graphite a final stage of anthracite, or of non-organic origin and a mineral? —Is the "link" between ape and man chronologically intermediate, or older than both of them? —Was Wallenstein only a *condottiere,* or did he intend to set up a unified State (corresponding to Britain and France) in Germany? There are many such alternative question-suppositions, setting the direction in which the probe must test for a response. In them, the suppositions *ante rem* are distinguished by their probing questioning from apparently related forms: from fictions and from hypotheses.

Scientific *fictions* first of all, such as the frictionless pendulum, Adam Smith's pure *homo oeconomicus,* and so on, are isolated and therefore—unlike suppositions—unchangeable auxiliary notions within research itself, and not so to speak *preceding* it for each newly apparent circumstance. Such fictions are deliberate simplifications; admittedly they are heuristically (though mostly only pedagogically) significant, yet being unrealistic from the start, they are neither denied nor confirmed by research. In the course of research, as when it has been brought to a relative conclusion, the frictionless pendulum in physics and *homo oeconomicus* in political economy remain exactly the same— quite unlike suppositions and their inquiring, anticipatory schemata.

The decisive difference between *hypotheses* and suppositions, on the other hand, is that hypotheses—though occasionally provisional—are *results* of investigation, and therefore in no way precede it. They occur in the inductive conclusion, and only as their empirical probability increases do they properly become results—the results of a *no longer hypothetical theory.* But of course, since all the individual instances are never known and known entire, even the conclusion, inductively and empirically obtained and confirmed on a wide basis, is only more or less substantially *probable;* hence, ultimately, no empirical result, no *vérité de fait,* emerges beyond mere hypothetical validation. Therefore it remains hypothesis—though always as a result, in contradistinction to the quite different situation of probing supposition.

At best the unfortunate term "working hypothesis" seems to approach supposition; it is a mixture of the two, but of course also a concession—a tribute paid by inductions to a foregoing supposition without which they could in no way interrogate particulars with regard to their universal. A prelude, a phase of supposition, remains indispensable—inductively and empirically as well: a foreplay of the "experimental thought" Mach posited

101

for recurrent physical phenomena; an exercising of the "ideal type" Max Weber suggested for non-recurrent historical phenomena. Even positivists recognize a beginning—a formal foreland of supposition. Even though, once it has served their purpose, the positivists put supposition away again; for pure empiricism (though a non-god) is a jealous -ism.

"EXPERIMENTAL THOUGHT" AND THE "IDEAL TYPE"

Marking and making a thing out to oneself (this at least) is necessary where something is to be explained, when something is to be understood. It is exacted by an inquiry that is not content merely to describe. Hence Mach recognizes the *thought-experiment* which must precede every real experiment. —Even if knowledge (as Mach believed) were nothing but the "adaptation of thought to facts." But, also according to Mach, scientific explanation to oneself varies in still suspended supposition by means of considered "guessing of the thought that is most appropriate in terms of mental economy." This method of deliberate conjecture is opposed to mere elementary trial and error: "Every experimenter," says Mach, "must have in mind the calculation to be carried out, before he translates it into action" (*Cognition and Error,* 1906). Despite the physicist Mach's own hardly impressive success with this kind of translation into "action," Galileo is certainly a prime exemplar of the practice of experimental thought. Without a thought-experiment, the movement of a chandelier would have conveyed nothing to him; and without his prior and appropriately directed inquiry, the famous falling apple would have told Newton nothing about gravity. Evidently Galileo filled the time between his intellectual investigation and physical experimentation with the suppositions of scientific "guesswork." (Of course, after empirical modification, all previous suppositions are excluded as mere conjectural has-beens. If they were false, now they are dangerous; if they were true, now they are superfluous and belong at best in the physicist's biography—not in physics itself.) Obviously the level of supposition is not absent precisely from reflective natural science.

The way in which supposition precedes true historical understanding is related to the foregoing. But there is a significant difference: in this case no real experiment can continue what was thought, as happens in the natural sciences. In addition, no historical process can be repeated, at least with the artificially produced and insulating conditions proper to experiments in natural science. And of course, purely in terms of the proper orientation of inquiry, the historian comes too late to his events. Yet supposition does have its place here too, in a specific form, and in testing an available though unrepeatable and variable sample.

The clearest instance of this is Max Weber's introduction of the concept of the "ideal type" into scientific social history. The ideal type is a provisional mental image of what, under conditions then obtaining, could possibly have happened at the specific time in question, and of the probable course of development. Weber the sociologist noted this peculiarly scholarly and scientific form of imagination, even though he was wholly an empiricist, a positivist as far as the theory of knowledge was concerned, and an especial enemy of all value judgments in science. He offers a "short-term ideal estimate" in order to compose processes of short duration, such as the Battle of Waterloo, in a single mental image that would make their data meaningful to the historian. Methodically, he postulates a "long-term ideal estimate" in order to provide a unified picture of long-lasting phenomena, such as the urban economy of the Middle Ages, the period of manufacture, or the interrelationship of capitalism and Protestantism. According to Weber, the only value obtained thus is heuristic: "The concept of the ideal type is designed to advance sound judgment in scholarly research. Although it is a hypothesis, it should indicate the *direction* that is appropriate during the formation of hypotheses . . . An ideal type is obtained by unilateral intensification of one or more view-

103

points, and by combining a profusion of given diffuse and discrete individual phenomena (more of the one or less of the other, and occasionally none at all) attached to the unilaterally selected viewpoints, in order to produce a unified theoretical image. Nowhere is this configuration actually to be found in such conceptual purity; it is a utopia.[?!] The task of historical science is to ascertain in each individual case how close to or distant from the ideal image the actuality may be . . . Such concepts are *mental* images in which we apply the category of objective possibility [i.e meaning that it could have been like that—but no more. E. B.] in order to construct contexts that our imagination, oriented to and informed by reality, deems appropriate" (*Collected Essays on Social Science,* 1922).

This is a remarkable and significant judgment, coming as it does from an empiricist. Even more remarkable (however reluctant the emphasis, and indeed wrong the orientation) is the dominant effect of the concepts of *utopia* and *objective possibility*. But enough of Weber's ideal types as a kind of thought-experiment in the field of the historical social sciences; as an historical counterpart to the mental model and conceptual model in the natural sciences.

From Mach, Duhem and Poincaré on, experimental thought (the atom model, the periodization model) has increasingly reinforced—though admittedly also restricted—the essential role of supposition. It has restricted it because a totally empiric and especially a positivistic use of supposition in the end wholly dispenses with that very supposition. It is a purely auxiliary construction before the facts, and once it has served its purpose it suffers the fate of that which is auxiliary—erasure. Neither experimental thought nor the ideal type is any longer in mind in the result obtained; both are rectified by matters of fact—essentially set right by *vérité de fait.* Apart from some measure of biographical interest, at best the history of the natural sciences offers a chance of preserving the conjectural model—on condition of course that it did at least tolerable heuristic service.

But Kepler's first law of planetary motion was preceded by the supposition that movement in a circle, as the "most com-

104

plete" form of motion, was the only one "fitting" for the planets. What of empirical value could be retained of this supposition? And what would remain of Kepler's harmony of the spheres, of this solely aesthetic-mythic "ideal type" in which (so he thought) there resounded the "harmony" of the universe—conceived quite literally? Nothing of value to be retained empirically, for the planets move not in circles but in elliptical orbits; and the harmony of the spheres could be kept at best as beautiful nonsense allowing of not even the smallest degree of adaptation (as the excuse for a concept of "universal beauty," for instance). But even if ultimately less ridiculous examples are chosen, indeed precisely when the assumptions have nothing to do with an older, qualitatively outdated cosmogony and are wholly quantitatively and empirically serviceable: even then both experimental thought and the ideal type are inductively and scientifically eminent only in the workshop, but not in the result.

Ultimately, scientific phantasy is valid only in its *cancellation* —as determined by the facts. It is the *only form of imagination which grows empirically wise through factual damage*.

It became apparent that suppositions—even when they had to be discarded subsequently—were inevitable. Indeed, they have their place in the formal syllogism itself. For the inductive experimental conclusion, which proceeds from the particular to the general, consists not of two, but of three terms; that is, it has a discreet major premiss. And precisely this, in terms of formal logic, provides room for the supposition—especially conspicuous here in the form of conjecture. Of course the inductive major premiss is a cryptogram: on account of the hasty disavowal of the bud, its flower has never bloomed. It is very different from the major premiss in the deductive syllogism: that supremely prominent premiss that is purely and simply apodictic, emphatically true. The secretly retained inductive major premiss, on the other hand, is far from being ready to affirm that all men are mortal, and therefore alone enjoys the mode of problematic judgment, the mode of the judgment of possibility. Precisely as experimental anticipation, without which the par-

105

ticular cases to be investigated could never be appropriately enumerated and appreciated, let alone be "induced" in the direction of conjecturing a law ($\frac{g}{2}t^2$) or a formal arrangement (the order of battle at Waterloo). And (very important) the inductive major premiss remains cryptogrammatic because its pre-concept of the result which is to be obtained inductively and empirically has no specific status and value.

Accordingly: scientific imagination (far beyond the mere fortunate special case), considered empirically, is a form of imagination open to thought and application, to manipulation and self-manipulation. Therefore empirical science, with regard to experimental thought and the ideal type, blooms and flourishes as a form of reason that has grown wise through factual damage.

THE "PLUS ULTRA" OF PHILOSOPHY

Very different is that form of opining which imagines itself capable of continuing straightforwardly in its somewhat. That is, straight-forwardly, and therefore not with just any ideal images and wishful thoughts to be fitted to every external, whatever it may be. And not with prejudices from an earlier cosmogony which would be seen to be purely or at least predominantly ideological. Of course Kepler's musical harmony model of the universe also belongs to this realm of the overtaken and antiquated. But a *qualitative* category (and here also there is a connexion with Kepler) operates differently in such a conception of Nature, which does not *a limine* erase sound, color and qualities of value from it, and which therefore does not thoroughly quantify Goethean Nature.

And what about the great philosophical ideas to which the world of facts, as a positivistic world, allows no *placet* in pounds, shillings and pence? Is the Pythagorean correspondence of numbers and qualities (not quantities) wholly devalued? The long-lasting Platonic eros—the dialectic unity of not-having and having, of poverty and riches? The Aristotelian matter-form relationship—in which the form is impressed in the matter and, alive, continues to develop? The Kantian conception of ideas of the unconditioned to which no empirical experience corresponds? Is Kant's idea contradicted or even rendered meaningless because, *expressis verbis,* it goes beyond the limits of any empirical experience? Or, from a quite different viewpoint, is Schelling's idea of perspective (that Nature is the Iliad of the spirit, and history its Odyssey) in the same sense factually disposed of—above all, negatively or positively empirically verifiable? Of course not. Yet, because all the abovementioned "statements' of these "thought-experiments" or "ideal types" cannot be entirely adjudged true or untrue by observation, availability and facticity, positivism calls such major speculative suppositions particularly "meaningless." Accordingly Plato, Aristotle and metaphysics as a whole (the greater, the more surely) afford no more than "musical exercises" whose supposition never needs a moment's thought. But the case is notoriously different; and only philosophical colour-blindness pure and simple (not to speak of arrogance) could manage to patronize such far-ranging and soaring scientific imagination as "art" or—as the agnostics of the seventies said—as "intellectual fairy tales" or "philosophic romances." And this only because the Platonic teaching on eros extends far beyond motion as visible change of location, and Kantian moral philosophy far beyond an inventory of existing ethics.

In all these instances it is a question of what *ultimately* decides which opinion is purposeful. As if there were no difference between a supposition thought only for a short space of time and, as it were, a long-term supposition.

But let us take two general notions which initially would seem quite similar in the mere suspension and indecision of supposition: for example, the concepts "friend" and "professor"—two simple generic notions which are then logically accorded two somewhat inapt—and at best passively deprecatory—instances. Already a striking difference is apparent in the instance which decides the justness or unjustness of the correspondence. Say the following is asserted: "*X* is not a proper professor"; it is then absolutely necessary to consider from what kind of previous instances this concept of "professor" might be abstracted. Perhaps we are faced with a new kind, so that the previous notion of a professor has to be dissolved, and expanded empirically with new attributes. The suppositions in the inductive major premiss which point towards such a universal notion are and must be open to reason; not only is the old direction of interpretation rectified, but nothing stands in the way of its complete rejection. If on the other hand it is asserted: "*X* is not a proper friend," then the case is sensibly different: for no new variety of empiricism is an instance that gives the right to discard the "ideal type" "friend," to abrogate it in its direction as a moral postulate, and to enlarge it with the quite different fact. Here, on the contrary, the existing situation as it has come to be, i.e. the factual in the literal sense of fact (without *fieri*), has no right of decision over that which is "proper"; i.e., in this case, over the truth or falsehood of such *postulatory notions*. Not—certainly not—as if the ideal type designated in the postulate were static, or fixed and permanent (*sempiternus*), or even supra-historically eternal (*aeternus*). Admittedly the ideal types of the ideal are, in their *content,* wholly sociologically linked to the historically changing contents, and, as often, happen to bear with them (pharisaically) ideologies which are themselves only historic and worn-out. But the *direction* of such heedful postulative "ideal types" does not vary, thanks to that "ideal" in them which rectifies itself only in *fieri,* in *process,* and therefore not—in its being other than factual truth—by *the fact of that which is the case.*

Here it is in no way necessary that the specific, long-lastingly —i.e. ideally—charged supposition should at this level feature already a substantially adequate attribute-definition (*definitio*) in addition to its orientation-definition (*destinatio*).

It is absolutely unnecessary to know whatever the full positive content of the *humanum* may be, in order to recognize Nero as decidedly inhuman. Or, to adapt Spinoza's "*Verum est index sui et falsi*" (That which is true is a touchstone for falsehood and the truth) to the truth: *Hoc verum* (This which is true—

as this truth of the great moral suppositions and normative assumptions) *est nondum index sui, sed iam index falsi* (is not yet a touchstone for truth itself, but is already one for falsehood). Consequently we can make a negative statement, which *in this connexion* is so wholly unpositivistically possible: All the worse for the facts.

There is a maxim of verification which involved so little correspondence to the facts that it brought about the English, American and French Revolutions: "A thousand years of injustice do not justify one hour of them." This basic proposition arising from a consideration of the *humanum* intimately connected with morality, as presented by classical natural law, was wholly opposed to "verification" on the basis of nothing other than the political *status quo,* i.e. of injustice as it had come to be, as it was. Hence the difference between this and an accommodation of thought to facts is particularly clear; the illuminating *direction* of the humane postulate would direct rather than be directed by nothing-but-fact. —All the worse for the facts: which means in this case: *Philosophical* reason is not imagination that has grown wise through injury in such a way that it behaves only heuristically, and thus attains validity and prevails. Rather there is a primacy of "practical reason": that is, of the concrete *humanization* of all world situations and conditions, in the logic of philosophy as well. Then mere facticity has no right to interfere, for that right is possessed only by the tendency of the *process* and—especially—the latency of *objective-real possibility.* And so the indicated direction of humane supposition did not remain philosophically restricted to morality and its immediate context. Indeed, the right not to be a dog, this large-scale postulatory supposition with so little empirical confirmation, is not so very distant from some of the "intellectual fairy tales" of the great philosophies, insofar as the latter display sublime perfection in the completed initial-experiment. Spinoza's philosophy, conceived as the ideal type of a perfect cosmos, of a world where the sun of substance is at its zenith and where (to make the imaginative presentation adequate) no thing throws a shadow, is an essay in pantheism that certainly enjoys no empirical verification. Yet even here, next to the factual truth, there is (in this case unintentional) normative truth, even if no postulatory truth beyond the existent, no truth of the process towards such an optative world and optimum world (impossible in the case of Spinoza's staticism).

Yet crystal, strong and uniformally crystallizing, is thought suitable as a model to represent a world somewhat differently constituted (not only in "inadequate images") as geometrically deducible and as structurally complete. A mere optative, admittedly, yet with the claim to determine something utopian (crystal clarity) as existent. Nevertheless: the model as such (aiming at truth as sublimity) is not cut and dried, and belongs neither in a mere "psychology of world views" nor in a finished "pre-history of the empirical sciences."

But the notion of the model was used also for speculative outlines of very great import: for those which certainly— though unbeknown to themselves, and unreflectively—attempted a *utopicum* of what the world could be in its not empirically existent but in no way merely abstractly subtilized line of extension. Primarily as ethics, in postulative aesthetics, in the anthropological critique of religion and its latent core, philosophy is directed to this *plus ultra*. But is it not true that every major and centrally relevant cosmological metaphysics offers anticipatory designs whose essence cannot be annihilated by facts as they have come to be? They cannot be thus destroyed, because only in the world of becoming, in the world as a *concrete outline realm,* can they find their court of judgment—as a non-biased and uniquely concrete corresponding instance offered for rejection or for confirmation? Where the world itself is its own experiment, where the world itself produces *model forms* in its operative process, the philosophically constitutive imagination is *committed only to the representation and perfection of this fieri and its tendential-latent content.*

So much at this point about the methodic *plus ultra.* It need never capitulate before empirical method when the latter degenerates into a reified empiricism of facts; and of course it must never lose contact with *process*-empiricism, if its aspiration is not to become abstract eccentricity, and its ascent a descent. It must never lose contact, too, with its particular instances; for they are the opposites of reified facts, and therefore precisely the experimental moments of transition to that *plus ultra* with which genuine philosophical imagination—precisely as constitutive imagination—is allied.

"What, therefore, is operative and continually operative, according to the maxim 'This is the way begun, walk ye in it to its end,' is no longer a question of what things may be in any particular present moment, in their rules of empirical behavior and their scientific codification, but—with a different emphasis and the religious kind of non-renunciatory impulse—a question of what things, men and works are *in truth,* seen by the star of their utopian destiny and their utopian reality" (*Spirit of Utopia,* 1918).

"Possibility is the partial present existence of conditions, though a givenness that is never sufficient for their realization; it marks out the sphere in which nothing can be too beautiful, according to the conditions, not to be true in the future. The sphere in which the truth, precisely as a truth of essential being, with the full, very ancient, pure golden echo of being-in-truth, must in any case never be wary of being elevating . . . Precisely because things are not so, the guardian notion and its praxis operate just as untiringly during rectification as after it, as consideration of the *verum bonum,* the truly, supremely organized matter in sight" (*The Principle of Hope,* 1959).

It must be restated, precisely for the sake of the opining that is as particularized as it is centrally oriented: *Empiricism,* if not statically reified, and *metaphysics,* if not rising with a valedictory gesture to the world into the lifeless seclusion of the idea, are both inseparable from the shield, spear and eye of Minerva —the goddess of watchful industry, of diligence that looks far ahead. They belong together all the more surely, beyond all arrogance in the one case, and beyond empty aspiration in the other, when the philosophical *plus ultra* in the *creative* calculation arises and can arise from the same ground as in the *enlarging* dialectics of the *world.* Therefore verification in the object of the work, in the work of the object, need not be cancellation; on the contrary, very empiricism as well, not only makes a

111

contribution in its process, but in every step of progress makes its *own* contribution to what has, up to that point, come to be.

For not only thought can be experimental, but *world history itself is an experiment*—a real experiment conducted in the world and aimed towards a possible just and proper world. This kind of history is also an operative experimental probe, a *real-probe,* in countless *objective-real models,* in the direction of a still outstanding instance. Towards an omega instance as was always intended in philosophical anticipation: true being (*ontos on,* substance, full identity of appearance and essence). And so of course it is no fact but only an imperilled *fieri* of true being, with no ontology other than that of not-yet-being.

This *not-yet* first provides the self-changing process in the world and above all the changeable in the world with its flow and its plus—the situation of the being-before-itself of still objective possibility. However, the *fieri* comprehended with, in, and from this (possibility is the last-found category in the *plus ultra* of philosophy) occurs only as a lasting experimental extraction, model figuration and figurative model of outstanding true being. Therefore, experimenting and replete with experiments, the human *fieri* moves ahead: the advance of history, moving not in unilinear development but entirely polyrhythmically and polyphonically.

For the same reason, a possible governing reference point of the historical where-to is locatable only in a utopian and not in an already attained and established (well-established) field. There is only an unnegotiable *direction,* but there are many *testimonies and traits* in the experiment that is known as history, and in the laboratory that is the world.

15. Differentiations in the Concept of Progress

A GOOD CONCEPT

There are words that have an especially lucid effect in themselves. They speak clearly; they seem reliable. Their meaning, the concept they announce, seems so clear and straight-forward that they require no further debate. The concept of progress is a prime case in point; nowadays it is despised or respected according to the promise of one's situation. This materially radiant notion also has a formally lucid effect, as if its referent were particularly difficult to contend for but easy to understand. Hence the object of progress appears not only as luminous, but as a thing simple and clear in itself.

LOSSES ON THE MARCH FORWARD

Yet men have always known that all advancement is not advantage. Something can be lost in the process, as in the awakening of a child into adolescence, or of a youth into manhood. Something is disposed of as a man matures, but not always "set aside," which would be less culpable in the child and possibly more noble in the youth.

And, not materially comparable with the foregoing, yet so constituted that when a previous state is compared with the later condition, the former would seem very much more tolerable, in the process of social maturing too there is often matter for regret in the midst of rejoicing. An obvious example is the obscene condition of the working class in Britain during the undeniably progressive Industrial Revolution. Admittedly this misery was the precondition of the initial unleashing of the forces of capitalist production. Negation, complete dehumanization, was dialectically self-generated. Yet what a ghastly minus was characterized as progressive—"progressive" in the same sense as scurvy or tuberculosis. And this was not only a minus for the sake of the common achievement of a plus, but a genuine release of the forces of production in the midst of the plus. The entire nature of emergent capitalism is to be progressive—yet darkly progressive.

REGRESSION AND THE "HERALD'S STAFF"

At the same time the shadows are quite contradictory and therefore belong to the movement forward itself. But how can it be, if in the course of that progression which allows the positing of the afterwards and of that which will come later as that which will be better, if in progress, in an advance that is not merely numerical, this course brings *dead* reversals with it? That is, reversals that are not implicitly necessary dialectically, as in the case of the connexion between the increased misery of exploitation and the Industrial Revolution. To take the most hideous example, Hitler was by no stretch of the imagination the negation bringing socialism to final victory. And in this respect there is no certain chronological index of progress, by which what happens later in history is somehow or on the whole a progressive plus compared with what has gone before. If that seems a truism, well it didn't seem so to Hegel; for the Peloponnesian War after the age of Pericles, and the Thirty Years War after the Renaissance, put serious difficulties in the way of his concept of negation—otherwise wholly in the service of progress. And the thorn of this apparent truism can cut so deep that Rousseau—for the very sake of bourgeois-democratic progress —described all history to date, since the dawn of "inequality among men," as deterioration; and denounced the whole progression of civilization to date as a degenerate period compared with the happy primeval age of Nature.

An abstract and absurdly excessive condemnation, yet it registered proficiently the actual reversals of the advance: as against an abstract idolization of the passage of time in itself, by means of which the *time-fetishistic* ideology of progress in later social democratic thought postulated an automatic progress —a supposition based on the crude economics that could divine from an automatic growth of capitalism the "subsequent stage" of socialism. This kind of triumphalistic progressology did no service to progress, but rather harmed the real advance forwards; for the most part, it served only as the ideology of an

114

individual disinclination actually to be a cog in the mechanism of history. The plus sign, says Hermann Cohen (not inexactly), is the herald's staff of time; but mere time has often (and not always unjustly) been represented by the image of the hourglass—with sand running down and out, and the scythe nearby.

The plus sign as a herald's staff for the march ahead presupposes for objectively favorable times, for reversals, or for a campaign on tricky ground, men to bear it aloft. Otherwise progress—not comfortable, never formal—becomes no more than the fetish of duration for its own sake, and occasionally one capable of injury or crippling. —As with the Hitler period that followed or was even produced by the age that believed in an automatic *tout va bien.*

IRREGULAR DEVELOPMENTS IN THE TECHNOLOGICAL BASIS AND IN THE SUPERSTRUCTURE

But now we must turn to that time and that tract which are efficacious and informed with effort, and in which a movement forward is uniquely alive.

Here some (now pertinent) theoretical difficulties of the concept of progress appear, which require more precise differentiation. Now differentiation occurs quite materially in the object itself; it need only be philosophically portrayed (for of course philosophy is appropriate). Therefore a progress that is not dearly purchased at the price of misery (let alone of perversion) is not always uniformly apparent in the basis, and then in the superstructure. It is quite different in the functional group: the forces of production and conditions of production (economic basis) on the one hand, and the functional (not only reflex) group determined thereby—the superstructure—on the other hand. For, like the conditions, the forces of production can feature an advance with which the superstructure sometimes not only does not comply, but to which it is occasionally even opposed in terms of a particular cultural deficiency. A minor

115

though especially striking instance of this is apparent in the development of artificial lighting—as shown in a display of significant examples in a science museum. There was a long period of aesthetic and technical evolution from the pine-splinter and the clay lamp to the Roman or the Byzantine candelabra, and to those mosque lamps which are oriental fairy tales in themselves. And so on, with passable improvements, until the paths of technical and aesthetic progress that had been one for so long separated with the advent of the ever brighter though increasingly ugly oil lamp, the gas mantle which offered no more than a photometric brilliancy, and the filament lamp—at first only a crude glare but then made so acceptable with the aid of frosted glass or shades that its exceptional brightness now no longer dazzles the eyes. Yet, despite all this, even today a candelabrum set on an old mahogany table offers a more tender luminosity and a more convivial light.

A minor example, and one that cannot be pressed too far. Yet for a long time technical improvement and aesthetic development in lighting kept in step: there is no need to romanticize the case. Nevertheless, in the major and important matter—just at the point of intersection of technology and culture—there is Marx's famous diagnosis of what he calls "disproportionate development." In the Introduction to his *Contribution to the Critique of Political Economy,*[30] Marx refers to the lack of proportion between the high level of artistic achievement and the low level of technical development in ancient Greece, and to the reverse relationship in the modern capitalist era. According to Marx the great epic can be produced only at a relatively primitive stage of technology; consequently the nature of progress can be very different in the *forces of production* and in the cultural superstructure. Similarly, with regard to progress in the *relations of production,* i.e. the specific basis or infrastructure, in relation to the superstructure. Bach or Leibniz do not correspond in the least to the wretchedness of Germany at the time, which only, so to say, wet their feet, whereas on the other hand a fully developed state of capitalism could be damaging to the muses as well as to the masses. "Capitalist production," Marx says with special emphasis in his *Theories of Surplus Value,* "is inimical to certain branches of creative production such as art and poetry." Without this insight, without this separation of an economic and State evolution from a hardly so happy development of the epic, one would have "the fanciful imagination of the French eighteenth century which Lessing satirized so admirably." Again this implies that politics and art were not always intercommunicating channels with regard to the rising bourgeoisie. The material connexion between the determinative basis and the superstructure which it determines, and which has a reciprocal effect on it, is limited; obviously progress does not occur at the same rate and at a proportionate level of achievement in the basis and in the superstructure. And something else is supremely decisive with regard to the difference in levels of development, and with regard to the goal which is so essential to the category of progress throughout: As soon as a work is not only significant but continuously significant and therefore forward-pointing, in terms of its goal, it often goes far beyond the so-called "totality" of a society. Otherwise it would necessarily share in the desuetude of a past infrastructure, and also a partial (political) superstructure. Otherwise there would be no enduringly effective *cultural legacy*—which is a matter not of full-bottomed wigs (whether at a fancy-dress ball or on the stage), but of Bach and Leibniz; a matter not of the politics of Renaissance princelings, but of the culture of the Renaissance. Such major yields from what-has-been do not perish—in contrast to considerable areas of their infrastructure, and also of some superstructures. They are themselves taken up in a specific and still by far unsurpassed progress forward, with the continuing revelation of ever new aspects of their content. Therefore there is every reason to speak of disproportionate development in this respect too, i.e. of continuing development in *Werther,* but also of a development wholly locatable *contemporaneously* in Prussian common law *circa* 1794. And every reason as well to associate the accompanying superstructure of *Faust* or *Werther* or *The Magic Flute,* in accordance with its far distant or high set goal, with another form of progress,

117

should it happen to correspond with the mere transient harmony of the forces of production and productive relations.

ART IMPARTIAL; ART AS A BARRIER TO THE ADVANCE OF CULTURE

But again we encounter the doubt and hesitation that arose with the movement forward—or rather: not this time with the movement itself, but with new snares in its all too straight way. The aporias met with now arise primarily from new valuations of forms which had long been assessed as mere first steps to supposedly more proficient artifacts. For a long time Egyptian pictorial works of art were considered to be "crude" precursors of Greek creations; one reason for this was the assessment of Egyptian plastic art by analogy with the actually "inelegant" archaic art of Greece. Obviously the classical ideal of beauty provided the prejudiced standard of evaluation; from that viewpoint even Thorvaldsen[31] would seem to be an example of "progress" in comparison with the head of King Zoser from the Third Dynasty. And Oedipus' answer would have solved not only the riddle of the Theban but the secret of the Egyptian sphinx; and his answer was "Man!"—man in an exclusively Greek-classical image.

Nowadays this supposed progress from Egyptian to Greek sculpture no longer seems so obvious. The Egyptians, indeed, have been awarded a credit mark for the homogeneity of their sculpture. In place of the classicist devaluation of all non-Attic art, Alois Riegl introduced the concept of *Kunstwollen,* in the sense of the specific artistic intentions and formal problems particular to any great culture. (The point itself is hardly novel: the nexus of problems had already been raised in the eighteenth century by Richard Hurd in his *Letters on Chivalry and Romance* [1762], at the time of the initial re-encounter with Gothic art.) Later, Worringer (in *Abstraction and Empathy,* 1908) more than dubiously psychologized, dualized and irrationalized the concept of *Kunstwollen* (specific artistic intention); yet

118

Riegl himself (*Questions of Style,* 1893; *The Late Roman Art Industry,* 1901) was still blissfully unconscious of a reactionary mandate, and only the classicist schema had to give way. In the perspective of *Kunstwollen,* in the end even non-European art was elevated without any mediatization; the alleged supremacy of later Greek work over Egyptian sculpture (the "developmental theory") vanished. Greek art no longer appeared so unquestionably progressive in relation to Egyptian art; and this became the starting-point for consideration of new theoretical problems in the concept of progress itself. Shortly after Riegl, of course, the dilemma impinged on the declining bourgeoisie's interest in dismissing progress itself as an historico-philosophical category, and considering it unhistorical—in specific cultural matters at least. The multiform existing differences between technical and cultural levels of achievement were also exploited for this purpose, and entirely played up to the point of assuming a *non-historicity* of art and its intentionality.

Alfred Weber's sociology of culture belongs to the same movement. He does allow progress validity in the "social process" and in the technical-scientific "process of civilization," but the "cultural movement" that he would have as existing substantially beyond these "externalities"—outside this "casing" —would be discernible in "rhythms of life" quite different to those of progress as a process of totalization.

For Hegel, on the other hand, *history as a whole* consisted of "progress in consciousness of freedom"—which alone made it history. For Hegel, it was still a coherent human progress, in accordance with the basic axiom of his philosophy of history: *Tantae molis erat humanam condere gentem* (Such toil was required to establish the human race).[32] On the other hand, the "recovery"—so eminently meritorious in itself—of art that had hitherto been so undervalued (so-called primitive art as well) led ultimately, in the age of bourgeois decline, of antidemocracy, to the general arrestation of progress in culture. Not only the humanity of the Ninth Symphony but the unity of the human race (already posited by the Stoics, who conceived of progress as coherent, as a matter of universal history)

119

was retracted by Fascism. This despite the fact that the aporias of the concept of progress to date, the theoretical difficulties of a concept far too straight-forwardly applied to Europe, were and are a matter of the breadth of art history, *and* of the wholly representative and aesthetic intrinsic valuation of non-Greek and above all non-European art.

"CULTURAL SPHERES," GEOGRAPHISM AND A MULTIPLICITY OF VOICES

Other attempts are made to use the indisputably problematical for extrinsic ends. The dubious concept of *Kulturkreise* or cultural spheres—which extends far beyond Riegl—was applied to fine art in general. Consequently a new aporia appears in the concept of progress, one arising from its unilinearity, yet now related to the contradictions of a real universal history. It is the aporia of a deficiency of *historical space:* that is, the difficulty of accommodating the gigantic amount of non-European historical material in any adequate representation. Therefore the mere succession of progress (that European if not predominantly German time-axis applied by Herder, Hegel and Ranke—though with many simultaneous asides, or side-altars) is paid for anew. According to this theory, Babylon and ancient Egypt can be treated very simply as undoubtedly bygone cultures at the *beginning* of written history; yet this categorization seems inappropriate for China, India and so on, which—unlike Babylon—have not disappeared. Accordingly, in the case of ancient Egypt and Babylon as well, their extensive after-effects, their long-existing river bed and river system, are not adequately situated. The reactionary theory of cultural spheres certainly did not wish, *contre coeur,* to absolve China or India from this historical banishment—quite the reverse. Of course, it had affinities with arch-imperialist geopolitics and worked with the reactionary shading which in Fascism quite penetratingly required the words "area" and "form" before the undesirable process—term "time." Hence, in the case of Frobenius,

Spengler and other "morphologists," a kind of *geographism* prevailed in place of an all too unilinear *historicism*. It worked not with movements of progress but only with circumstances of biological maturation within the specific "areas of culture," and above all with ultimate symptoms of senility. Of course these separated processes were valid uniquely within the individual cultural spheres, not—so to speak—within the totality and for the totality of an historical process conceived of as a continuum. Accordingly, *symptoms of ageing* (but these alone) would be preordained for the whole of history—for its nihilistic last moments; and could be confirmed rather than removed by the splintering action of geographism.

This would mean a surrender not only of the Stoic concept of a united humankind, but above all of the Augustinian notion of a unified *history* of the human race. Moreover, the specific concept of the "process" of history would be dissolved—that concept with which the still rising bourgeoisie expanded the more conservative eighteenth-century notion of "progress." Expanded, that is, with a kind of historical chemistry that can be observed not only in the Romantic philosophy of Nature but in the philosophy of history, and especially in that of Hegel. For Hegel's notion of progress conceived of a "processing out" of content, as if there were the increasing gleam of a "silver vein" of essential being in the fermenting mass of the metal of history; and above all, for Hegel, this processing out would be ultimately uniform: with becoming-for-itself as the universally synthetical *unique goal*. But all this and more is missing from the doctrine of cultural spheres, from the attempts at cordoning off, and the supposed major islands (without any system of intercommunication) which Spengler's "morphology" above all spared from world history. Then not only Egypt, India or China would be a ghetto in itself, but Greece (with its "Euclidean cultural spirit") would be radically separated from the later West (with its "Faustian cultural spirit"). Of course the same isolating geographism was then offered as a broad and particularly accommodating *storage space* for all these cultures and their history. The latter was assessed purely according to the analogy

121

of childhood, youth, manhood and old age; therefore time—
somehow still undeniable—was itself related to a "sphere"; with
a now permissible juxtaposing or co-existence of *several cultures*. Hence time, like the life of organisms, would become
cyclic, and progress would be made to describe an ultimately
entirely repetitive curve. But because such curves or cycles
almost without limit would be juxtaposed on the earth without
any precedence and subsequence, even without any necessary
togetherness, even this geographically divisive spatial categorization is a static obstacle to an historically progressive categorization in time. Accordingly, the aporia which resulted from the
unilinear succession of time as far as the reception or insertion
of the historical (and particularly the non-European) material
was concerned, would be avoided, indeed—so to speak—removed. But by recourse to a truly drastic measure: the demise
of the coherent process of history itself, which unites countries,
people and epochs.

Nevertheless, even here the adversary calls our attention to
something which progress immediately deprives him of. As with
Kunstwollen and its consequences, here too (if "space" is not
poisoned) an implication can emerge quite different to that
envisaged by the advocates of cultural spheres. They would
divide history into sectors, islands and autarchies, and artificially
mark off a construction that is already extremely artificial. Then
at best history would look like a circus with three or more rings,
where—simultaneously—acrobats perform, horses show their
paces, and the fire swallower displays his skill, but all in isolation. Or historical time, because it does not assist the doctrine
of separate spheres of culture, and is not sufficiently functionless
and aimless, is transformed into a group of formally measured-
off circular mountains; and history becomes a lunar landscape.
Reactionary geographism does not offer any perspective beyond
this; from start to finish it is empowered only to destroy the
impulse of progress and its concept. Nevertheless (and this is
a kind of rational stratagem) the category of space (here both
disfigured and exaggerated) *has no difficulty* in accommodating
the immense historical material of the earth. It is therefore a

question (once the theory of cultural spheres has been tried and found wanting) of allowing a kind of *subsidy of space in the chronological line of history*—quite without reference to the interested statics of geographism. In other words, it is a question of considering whether, *within the wholly processual succession of history,* at least as many simultaneous or chronologically successive settings are not needed and demonstrable as, say, are required to provide an appropriate straightness of execution in epic art. Admittedly, the events portrayed in different settings in the great epics are interwoven with great artistry, whereas Europe and India—and even China—did not (or virtually did not) communicate with one another for thousands of years; and the stages of social development of the various nations of the earth are hardly "simultaneous." Nevertheless the postulated multiplicity of voices is possible: a methodic profusion, an interweaving of time and of epochs, and therefore a spaciousness in the flow of history, which would in no way necessitate any recourse to geographism.

If the lack of, or disrupted, communications between nations, and above all the different stages of social development, should happen to effect a separation, there is no resulting disturbance to the uniform movement: a symphony (to introduce a methodically apt formal analogy) does not feature a *continuo* of all voices—on the contrary. In the case of all breaks (and is there any reality without a break?) the uniformity of procedure and performance is already guaranteed by the uniform regularity of the social development and the never absent relationship of basis and superstructure. Everywhere there is an advance from a primitive commune, through class societies, to the ultimate maturity of socialism; and everywhere, in all ensembles of social relations, there is the human element—from the anthropological to the *humanum*—which colors these ensembles so variously, and holds them in a uniform embrace. Undoubtedly so polyphonically cohesive a picture is much more difficult in the case of universal history than in that of periodization; in universal historical terms, at least, it requires a *multiverse*—and chronologically too. But the concept of progress hardly founders with this productive complication: in utter contrast to geographism with its stationary and stagnant effect.

The occurrent and existing multiverse of cultures is itself evidence that the *humanum* is still in the process of becoming conscious of its freedom and selfhood; that it is not yet discovered, but sought for and experimented for everywhere. *Therefore this humanum (still in process), together with the many experimental, explorative and contributory paths towards it, provides the only genuinely tolerant (i.e. utopian-tolerant) point of time.* And the more nations and cultures belong to the humanist camp, the larger and surer will be the reality and therefore the conceivability of a single goal for the multiverses in the new history of culture.

A "FLEXIBLE" TIME STRUCTURE IN HISTORY, ON THE ANALOGY OF RIEMANNIAN SPACE

Time *is* only because something happens, and where something happens, there time is. But not enough thought is given to the matter of whether and how far the variant "that" of that which happens, proclaims itself in the variant form of its flow. This is quite clear in the case of time that is merely experienced— at least with regard to subjective (often all too subjective) perception and ideation. Here the perception of time (for reasons that need not be adduced at this point) is quite different in effect from the representation of time—i.e. inversely. A lively hour passes quickly, but a dreary one creeps by; in memory, on the other hand, hours that have been enlivening, or "great" days, expand considerably, whereas entire months of dreariness contract in reminiscence to the point of nothingness. But of course this varying estimate of a flow of time that is always the same in content in each specific case shows that mere experience-time still cannot provide a satisfactory resolution of our problem. For this subjective representation refers only to the *length* of the occurrence, exactly as in the case of time-by-the-clock—

time wholly external. Here, at the most a substantial, qualitative distinction is indicated—one between "empty" and "full" time. Yet there is something here that is not represented by conventional, clock-measured, non-subjective, formal-metric time. But in clock-time, of course, the changing and above all inconsistent units of mere experience are absent. *Clock-time* is uniformly divided and proceeds in equal periods; it advances "inexorably": that is, uniformly. Hence it can be expressed by a numerical progression, which makes both the clock-face and the calendar possible. But the form of progression denoted in this way is *wholly indifferent to the contents which occur or do not occur within it.* Time-by-the-clock is abstracted from time-as-it-is-lived, and also made abstract; it wholly rectifies time lived, but at the price of formal rigidity. This inflexibility is indispensable in order to measure time—and for working time (even though this may also be qualitatively evaluated in a different way), for historical chronology, for the terms of validity of legal contracts; as the foot-rule is to the spatial arts, so the metronome is to the arts of time. But clock-time never indicates "emptiness" or "fulness," as still semi-quantitative determinations of density: for time-by-the-dial is always uniformly dense. Or, as abstract time, it is everywhere uniformly empty, together with its advance or progression itself, in which—evidently—no qualitative progress is indicated intrinsically. Not even a "relentless flow" is shown by the formal ticking on of clock-time, for then contents from a quite different realm are included.

The Marschallin in the *Rosenkavalier* stops all the clocks at night because they record time, and time runs down towards old age and death; this action superimposes age and time on the movement of the hands just as a tin *memento mori* with a perpendicularly moving scythe is attached as an ornament to some baroque clocks. And if it is true that the wheel of history, in the long run at least, cannot be turned back, then this wheel means the addition wholly of *tendential time* (even though it is a figure drawn from the clock wheel; and even though this retains the positive forward motion of the clock-wise clock's hand), and is therefore a very qualitative time, and not an intrinsically neutral clock-time.

And even if clock-time, as that of chronology, is necessarily at the basis of every historical-substantial time, at best it is not much more than the rigid skeleton beneath the flesh and blood of tendency-time. If clock-time is absolutized, it is a counter-concept to every attempt to conceive of the form of time on occasion (that is, when its contents require it) as non-rigid, even as "flexibly" as the new, no longer purely Euclidean physics grasps and comprehends space under certain micro- and above all macro-conditions. Clock-time, on the other hand, beats continually with the same chronometric rhythm, showing forth the abstract, simplest form of coherent succession of the uniform one-after-the-other. And much more than mere *rubato,* and a mere change of tempo, is necessary to deal fittingly with *historical time and its "times."*

Initially, the question of time in inanimate yet impelled matter seems a simpler problem. Because it is quantitative, this measurement concurs with the uniformly constant succession of numerical progression. And, physically, time plays not in the remotest way the same role as space—so long conceived of as typically uniform. It did not play this role even for Galileo, who concerned himself with the calculation of non-uniformly accelerated motion. And not for Newton, for whom time as t was only a quantitative representation of a variable independent of events, which "of itself, and from its own nature, flows uniformly without regard to anything external," in order to permit numerically exact limit transitions. An essential feature of historical time is exactitude of orientation-irreversibility, and this has always been absent from the equations of physics. Only the second law of thermodynamics, which treats of so-called "entropy" in a closed system, recognizes irreversible orientation in the concept of time—analogously expressed in a *non-equation;* but this second law, the postulation of entropy, is also the most anti-structural of the major laws of physics.

The new physics of the relativity and quantum theories has

126

treated the category of time from entirely new viewpoints, above all in terms of Einstein's critique of the Newtonian presupposition of a simultaneity of all—even the remotest—events. As is well known, simultaneity exists (at least with differences so minute that they can be ignored) only for adjoining positions, but is not transportable through large tracts of space. Therefore very far distant places do not enjoy a simultaneous moment; and not only on account of the non-*measurability* of this simultaneity (which in any case would be exclusively an operative-idealistic and not a factual-real confirmation). Every place, according to Einstein, has its own specific time—at least with regard to the moment. However: although the theory of relativity got under way with time problems ("point events") and the quantum theory is also full of them (time only in the case of an aggregate of quanta, not in the case of the individual effective quantum), it remains true that time precisely is ultimately declassed (and indeed from the start) in the first quantized and then mathematized concept of Nature found in physics. As not particularly prominent one-dimensional time, it is connected with the three dimensions of space, and, in four-dimensional multiplicity, produces no asymmetry. Each "world point" ("now" and "here") is determined by its combined space-time co-ordinates x_1, x_2, x_3, x_4; but—inclusively of the temporal "co-ordinate axis"—these co-ordinates are only numbered values, and time is not distinguished from them by any special characteristic. Ultimately, this means that in physics there is no question of specifically *natural-historical time as the mode of being of a tendential event.*

But the case is different with *space conceived in so novel and flexible* a manner, although in it time precisely is declassed by total mathematization; and the concept of space of the new physics is very closely related to its concept of time. However, it is not this relationship (with an a-historical, pure mechanical time) that is in question here, but only the variable metrics itself —no longer Euclidean and therefore applied to space above all. Therefore, precisely on the basis of flexibly conceived *Riemannian space,* it is possible to conceive of something

127

analogous that would assist the formation of a *non-rigid concept of time in history*. It would assist this concept in the midst of its progress aporias and (closely related to these) the aporias of the allocation and classification of historical material.

Riemannian space is not intrinsically rigid, but rather variable; it allows of changes in its proportions: not on grounds of pure operative-idealistic calculation, but overwhelmingly for objective reasons. Accordingly, Riemann assumed objectively (thus giving "room" for the theory of relativity) that the metric field is not rigidly given once and for all, but depends causally on matter and changes with matter; therefore the *field* does not adhere to a static homogeneous form, but to the form of *changeable events*. Although extensions and complications of Einstein's theory of relativity still have to be proven, the *objectively variant distribution and movement of matter* in the universe itself conditions non-Euclidean variable metrics. This is significant in terms of a permissible—indeed a requisite—analogy for the *concept of historical time,* precisely because *the historical material is diversely distributed.* Therefore, in contrast to the concept of space of modern physics, the sphere of plasticity—of visibility—is not relinquished; and the analogy (as is methodically concordant) provides only a preliminary pointer: in any case, one may refer from a natural space to an historical time only with considerable qualifications. Conventional history, however, does not recognize the *problem of* variable dimensions of time, let alone that a non-rigid concept of time itself might be called for on the basis of the *variant distribution of the historical matter.* The four-dimensional space-time world, as conceived of by modern physics above all for "macrocosmic"—i.e. astronomical—conditions, is certainly not so constituted that time flows within it as a mode of being of processually substantial motion. Physical time (with the exception of that of entropy) lacks all characteristics of orientation, even a merely conceivable non-recurrence. Nevertheless, in this respect precisely, the *space of physics* can teach time something: namely, that in its historical succession, time likewise is conceivable *suo modo* as inconstant, and if not as curved, at least as "rich in curves." A "multi-dimensionality" of the time-line, as demanded above all by the geographical richness of the historical material, is of course wholly foreign to physics itself. However lavish it may be in n-dimensionals, "time-space," in the union of time and space, profits little thereby. Whenever *history, or natural history, reappears in physics,* a quite different "elasticity" would be necessary here as well, in order to represent the course of flow as a variable form of varying movements, of cosmogonic developments.

As far as *human* action is concerned, a mere division into different times (ages) has been found satisfactory. Of course these fragments are given different names—Antiquity, the Middle Ages, Modern Times—just as if they stood for different hues of time; as if different kinds of time were already in use here which corresponded with the substantial events of such periods. Yet this coloring remains purely external and peripheral; it is a mere tinted impression of what begins or ends *socially* at the epochal limit in each particular case. In this terminology, in spite of all attempts at divisions, time itself remains chronologically the same; at most something like human age is transferred to it by analogy—the Greek adolescence of the human race, and so on. Also there is a vapid sort of pinpointing, a kind of inference of renewal in a phrase such as "the dawning of a new century"—to say nothing of mystical emphases once placed on numbers (the year 1000, and 1524). But it is highly significant that not the recording of history as continuity, but the "special disciplines" of historic being and consciousness, which belong to history as a whole, have long made use of individual and *legitimate* time structures. Above all there is the very important economic concept of working time, in which the same hour is given a variant assessment according to the work performed qualitatively in it in each particular case, and is credited as a multiple.

And there are also quite individual time structures in the superstructure: here one need only mention musical and verse *rhythms*—and in particular the *structural divisions* of music. There is a poised or calm time in the fugue, and a tense time

129

in the sonata—that is, one allowing room for tensions. There is a broad, onward surging, exceedingly spacious time in the epic, in contrast to time in drama, which is quite materially (not artistically) compressed, or curtailed, or skipped over, or overlapping. In the structure of the sonata as in that of the drama, there is also an individual dominant-tonic-relationship of its own specific time, which takes the no longer chronic but acute, because specifically serviceable, procedural form of blow-upon-blow or stroke-after-stroke of the approaching, then—as it were—vertically striking fall or victory.

Indeed, entire *cultures* not only stand in time, in the sense of their period, but themselves contain, pre-eminently in their mythology (or religion), a specific time which participates in their individual cultural forms of time—in this respect one need only mention the almost futureless Greek mode of time, and the eschatologically rich Christian mode. And Greek mythology has its time gods, who are—analogously—special gods of motion: Eos, Nike and Hermes—all winged. But what a difference when compared with the "time god" Yahweh; when he, full of *futurum,* defines his name thus to Moses: *"Ehje ascher ehje"*— "I will be what I will be."[33] And again, in so to speak a more earthly *consecutio temporum* (not only in the case of John the Baptist but in that of Thomas Münzer), what has *kairos*-time— a time that is "secure in itself," that is "fulfilled"—in common with the unemphasized time of the Greeks, or with the unending movement onwards that Hegel called "base eternity"?

Item: There are varied time structures—not in the simple chronology of historical succession (which is related only to clock-time), but in the above-mentioned time-color problem of individual historical *periods,* and, above all, in a legitimate way, in the individual *superstructures.* It is these varied time structures which—as aforesaid—do not allow progress in economy, technology and art to be attributed simply to the same common denominator. Therefore it is also evident that among the multifarious material which varies the form and content of the concept of historical time and makes it accordant with the particular material, there is ultimately to be found the still manifold *material of the goal,* to which in terms of value the forward movement of the various time series is in each case referred and directed. Precisely these teleological relations and references, which are not yet wholly inter-homogeneous, bring about variations not only in the different types of progress—but in the time structures in which these different, so often non-uniform types of progress (in economy, technology, art and so on) occur. The totality of the particular social tendency—also as the total particular time-tendency—certainly overtakes the temporally layered spheres of movement of this tendency; yet the different layer-flows (that is, the movements of different levels) persist in the outreaching whole. And they require most especially to be approached with considerations of time-content that are no longer merely homogeneous—they demand a *kind of* *"Riemannian" time.* That is: a time with a variably conceivable metrics—varying according to the particular division, and above all according to the (still variously distant) teleological contents of the historical matter.

Leibniz also allowed time, and not only space, to be comprehended as an operative form of forces and their movement, and type of movement. This is a dynamic conception of time; hence it does not see, in their consequence, the time series of human history too as unalterable and wholly similar in construction. Moreover it sees a *difference* between the millions (to say nothing of the geological or cosmological milliards) of years of pre-history and the few millennia of *cultural history* since Neolithic times. Here not only a chronometric difference but one of density in the being of time itself, above all a qualitative-structural distinction, holds sway: in short, an objective changeability in the before-and-after sequence as well. This occurs in every *overtaken unity of the developmental-historical relationship;* it is not a chronologically linear but a chronologically *differentiated* and *federative* and only thus fruitfully *centered* relationship.

But of course one must remember that there are no intrinsic times or forms of time—times-in-themselves. There is no arguably different metrics *apart from* the social life of its "time"—

as if a time structure lived and changed as such. No more than there is pure clock-time in history or (which comes to the same thing) time as an abstract-neutral container. Such a form of time can be postulated only because of the unthinking convention that arises solely by reason of the difficulties of accommodating the universal-historical material. —Or perhaps because of a reactionary variety of static interest, as when Nikolai Hartmann asserts that time is always time, and remains so whatever happens within it. Unlike the historical consciousness, the philosophic consciousness may not "confound extension and dimension: whatever 'extends' in time is never time itself," which instead elapses indifferently (*Philosophy of Nature,* 1950). But for all that, Hartmann's prohibition is instructive in revealing formalism and categorial statics as the only decisive counter-position to Leibniz and variable consequences. From the static viewpoint, differentiations in the concept of progress, and time *seriatim,* must seem unnecessary or ridiculous according to circumstances.

In addition—to go beyond the reactionary kind of static interest—all unconsidered habituation to clock-time displays certain affinities with a separation of so-called formal logic from dialectics—in this case in the theory of categories itself. For the reification of chronometry would also remove the dialectical transformation which, as such, is as inescapably characteristic of the concept of time as of any other notion which conceives of processes (and what concept other than that of time represents more genuine processes?). Hermann Weyl compares Riemannian space, as distinct from rigid-Euclidean space, to a "fluid . . . a mobile location and orientation yielding to active forces" (*Philosophy of Mathematics and Natural Science,* 1927). Would this variability be less appropriate to the *panta rhei* of time? Here there is no n-dimensional multiplicity, as in a wholly non-graphic geometry: what must be noted is the purely graphic, historically and materially requisite multiplicity in which the chronological variations occur.

Therefore progress itself does not advance as a homogeneous succession of events in time; it moves forward on different levels of time that are below and above one another. It proceeds in a *humanum*-unity of passing and gain that is still only processing itself out in diverse ways. The really common uniform time of the process of history and, indeed, of the world process, springs and is springing forth universally only as a temporal form of emergent identity: that is, of non-estrangement between men, and of non-alienation between men and Nature. But apart from this horizon problem, the relationship of time (precisely as "pure restlessness of life," as Hegel calls it in the *Phenomenology*) to its varying contents is not one of unvarying externality. As the continually open mode of existence of material movements and processes, it participates in them flexibly; and it is specifically and materially determined by such movements and processes, both in periods and in areas of culture.

PHYSICAL AND CULTURAL SERIES, AND HOMER'S SUN[34]

If there is time only where something is happening, what if very little happens, or the something happens only with incredible slowness? Or does a succession which, so to say, counts only itself and in itself, and within which almost nothing changes, really proceed in the same way as in a time which is replete with events and "historical"? In other words: Is the time in which the murmuring surge unnumbered times on the same unnumbered idle pebbles chafes, and the time in which century after century hears the grating roar begin, and cease, and then again begin, really only longer or just as *dense* as one bare Russian 1917? And of course all these questions must be taken in a purely objective sense—not as questions solely about the time of human experience beyond the geological millennia. All epochs—not only those which are humanly historical—have to be comprehended in relation to the differentiations in the density of historical and material occurrence, of its tendencies and contents. There is also an intensive and qualitative difference between *historical time itself* and natural time (particularly that

133

in which the "history of Nature" occurs); a time other than that characterized by the t-components of physics. It is now apparent (though, of course, a quite different aspect will become evident shortly) that, despite its formally so very much longer duration, natural time is *less dense* than *historical-cultural time*. Though hugely inflated in comparison with the latter, natural time contains less intensive-qualitative time—just as pre-human Nature also contains less developed being. And its millions and thousands of millions of years, which are laid out in an apparently homogeneous succession before the few thousand years of human history (or appear exclusively so to extend), are accordingly—to use a slightly strained though appropriate metaphor—a kind of period of inflation compared with the gold period of history and culture—an inflation-age against a gold-age. Even the formally so much longer duration of natural time, because it extends before human history, is longer only according to *the mode of the past,* but not according to the *mode of the future* which, as generally supposed, is wholly predominant in human history. At least insofar as the latter appears as the only unconcluded form of history: the history of Nature pure and simple being substantially complete, despite its everlasting motion from incandescent vapor to incandescent vapor, or from cold dust to cold dust; and on account of this merely cyclic, therefore substantially concluded motion. For the cycle from primal haze to suns and planets (and on these, perhaps, the evolution of life in several forms) would include within each particular process (or, rather, from the appearance of the first traces of life to ever recurrent *nova*) no *novum* for the inorganic processes and certainly none for the vapor cycle. Stereotyped, unfruitful, all this would wreathe and wind about, enclosed within itself, as if it were wholly before human history—even if it were ultimately to bury human history beneath it, by drawing it back. Therefore, from the viewpoint of a "pre-historical" Nature pure and simple, dense, rich historical time appears as a plus in contrast to an inflated, natural time virtually inert to process.

But of course this presupposes that the time of so-called dead things must lie exclusively before human time. And that, like that which occurs within it, natural time must be *pure past,* having no more specific novelty concealed within itself. Only thus can it lie actually before human history: as a husk from which the grain has been taken; as a slave whose duty is done and whose capacity is exhausted; prodigious pre-history, but prodigious in no other way. Only thus does the history of Nature make a unilinear advance into the history of mankind, which succeeds it and "crowns" it historically, in development. Accordingly there was once a popular scientific book entitled *From the Nebula to Scheidemann* (O Scheidemann, core and crown of history now revealed!). But even if we substitute a more significant name, a cultural-historical effect always blocks off the natural-historical *prius,* allowing it re-entry only as a *prius* that is past: that is, as an exhausted mechanical uterus that might at most now idle on without function. Therefore a specific or— better—a positive future still appropriate to human history is no longer part of the natural transmission of matter. *Physis* can even be recognized as basis, and—from a purely cultural-historical viewpoint *ante rem*—in a blind alley of having-beenness.

But here one is reminded of a *similarly false* time-past in cultural history itself: the location to which Herder, Ranke and (*in toto*) Hegel assigned the Near-Eastern civilizations, above all India and China. Hegel saw the last two as no more than the earth and the rest of Nature immersed in the past—even though they still existed, and at that time their influences were felt quite contemporaneously. But for the developmental philosophers of the time, on the line of progress, Nature—and especially inorganic Nature—was, with "voice extinguished," virtually the sputtering done-for beginning. Hegel, for whom Nature was wholly subordinate to history, also asserted that the inorganic world was entirely precedent and exclusively past: "History came to the earth at an earlier time, but now that life which fermented in itself and possessed time in itself is arrested; the Earth spirit not yet in opposition—the movement and dreams of a sleeping entity before it awakes—achieves full consciousness in man, and now confronts itself as the peaceful figure it was." Thus Hegel describes the most decisively characteristic and assertive human point of history, which surpasses and renders obsolete the universe pure and simple. Since Nature accordingly becomes a mere prelude, its time must appear *wholly* non-compact and substantially inadequate—as it was represented in the first phrasing of the question.

And now the *second, supplementary* version: Is Nature in human history really *raised upon so ancient a plot,* that is, upon a time-plot locatable quite to the rear of mankind? Isn't it absurd to assert that Nature is past and done with in the same way, say, as the Crusades, and that like the Crusades and other events of times gone by, it persists at most in a few after-effects? What about the quite obvious and continuing relationship between men, *and between men and Nature?* And the relationship between men and raw materials, natural forces and their laws? And the aesthetic bond—together with all the questions of natural beauty and the myths of Nature that so often still resound in it? Doesn't Homer's sun shine on us too—and (quite apart from all connotations of the "legacy of culture") precisely as the actual sun itself that shows no sign of being outworn by human history? Wouldn't it be really absurd to maintain that the vast moving universe and its motion, wholly unmediated with us in the multitude of its stars, has its "continuation" *pure and simple* in the *existing* history of mankind, and has achieved its substantial goal in existing cultures? So that the "Iliad of Nature" would literally have found its home and termination in the human "Odyssey of the Spirit"; and, accordingly, the time of the previous history of Nature would appear empty, and—in contrast to the time of human history—without any noteworthy future mode of its own? And therefore without progress *sui generis,* without real possibility in regard to that very far distant future, still so distant from *given* history; in regard to that profundity which as yet can hardly even be probed, and which *Marx* so recently pointed to as the humanization of Nature?

Consequently, in natural time as well, it is evident that in a truly universal-historical topology of times, consideration must be given to the problem of an *individual* natural succession of time that *does not wholly pass over into the given succession of history.* The single-file succession of before-and-after is least of all tenable as a not merely finished *before* of Nature, and a not merely all-expressive *after* of cultural history. Similarly, to conceive of the immense (and tense) structure of Nature as a setting against which the corresponding drama of human history has yet to be enacted, is more appropriate than to see human-historical being and consciousness already as the opened eye of all natural being; of a natural being which not only lies before our history (and bears it), but which for the most part continues to environ it as a history that is still hardly reconciled, in form or content, with historical time. —Assuredly not as a history that would have to remain absolutely unreconciled with natural time and with the particularly latent contents that acquire time within Nature's time. And consequently in a clear double entry of a goal of history and progress (the "common-wealth of freedom"), on the one hand, and a termination of the cycle of Nature ("entropy"), on the other hand. This dualism may seem far-fetched, yet it is a threat precisely where Nature is seen exclusively as the "before" of history that ultimately buries—in hot vapor or cold dust—the historical epochs that are certainly vastly superior to, yet in no way reconciled with or flowing into and ending in, natural time. —Ultimately buries, that is, in the sense that it brings them back in a mere "before-as-after," and a mere "after-as-before."

Therefore theoretical difficulties in the postulation of a prosperous and true developmental history are apparent here too, in natural, historical time; here precisely these aporias arise from the two abovementioned *aspects* of natural time: from a terminated *past,* and a largely inaugurated *tomorrow* of Nature. Relatively empty, futureless natural time on the one hand, and substantial natural time, replete with future, on the other, are both given—and not merely as methodic but as complementary, *actual aspects.* One is in the mechanical actual aspect of the past and its correspondingly quantitative, constant element; the other is in the anticipatory actual aspect of a dawn and whatever may correspond to it in the qualitative, open, symbolic element of

137

natural processes, conceived of primarily in the Goethean and not in the Newtonian sense.

The two modes of time do not, however, flow simultaneously yet separately; and the second does not simply cancel the first, *pro rata* valid mode: instead, both natural times are polyrhythmically *enwreathed in one another.* Consequently the *natural time of the dawning morrow-to-come,* as a time of the humanization of Nature, *is particularly bound up with the tendential contents of cultural historical time.* This also means that the real "Golden Age" of historical anthropology cannot be conceived of without the just as real "Golden Age" of a new humanist cosmology—one, therefore, which has *humane historical time* as its influential "before" and, accordingly, also realizes history *in natura,* in a positive-and-possible way—in a world mass—rather than entombing it negatively-and-possibly.

PROGRESS AND THE "MEANING" OF HISTORY

Clearly the summons to advance is as little finished with and in itself as the thing it indicates. The concept of progress implies a where-to and a what-for; a what-for to be willed, and therefore a good one; a what-for to be contended for, and therefore one that is not yet achieved or given. Without its whither and wherefore, progress is not conceivable, not measurable at any point, and above all not present in any way as the thing itself. However, the "what-for" implies not only a "goal" but (not simply coincident therewith) a purpose; and (again not simply identical therewith) a "meaning" to the process—at least to the humanly striving and working process. The so to speak automatic process, indeed life itself, just in order to be a process, requires no meaning (men do not live primarily in order to live, but because they live). But certainly the process and life willed, conceived and pursued as progress, neither emerges without a meaning, nor occurs without one; and to deny the reality (even though it is not yet a reality *realized*) of a meaning, is essentially to remove the conceptual and material content of progress. By saying that the meaning is not yet *really* realized, is meant that the meaning of the willing of progress and of the world in which that willing has a meaning, is contained not in a static given existence but in objectively real possibility, and in the dialectical tendency towards realization in the direction of that possibility. Meaning, therefore, is perspective to the extent that it is possible in the world which is to be changed; to the extent that, in the perfectibility of the world—the world's capacity of fulfillment—it possesses the latency of good aims. This perspective dawns gradually before the thinking and doing of what is actually needful; but the whole (*totum*) of what is absolutely needful must always be intended and remembered in this thought and action, so that both meaning as perspective and perspective as meaning may be present.

The same is evidently true of all that lies round about; true of the whole of history, of the whole meaning of the world. And always as a meaning that is not statically given but progressively to be brought forth by men—"This is the way begun, walk ye in it to its end!" Of course, if the surrounding consciousness of, and the consciousness of being surrounded by, such a utopianly really established meaning (a meaning at least not yet thwarted by any form of total purposelessness), are absent, then the individual and specific meanings of historic progress are without ultimate support and without a philosophical seriousness— namely, one that can be represented in a universally systematic way. If the world were basically only a mechanism and its "entropy," then history would be like trout fighting or making love in a tank whilst the cook without is already advancing from the door, bearing with her the knife disparate to yet destructive of the whole process in the tank.

The meaning of human history already there from the start is the building of the commonwealth of freedom; yet, without a positively-possible, possibly-positive meaning in the *surrounding cosmology* which all historical events ultimately merge with, the progress of this historical process (at least to a steady gaze from the viewpoint of totality) might as well never have happened. Of course, a single day can be spent quite meaningfully; a life

139

put to good—even productive—ends has its meaning, above all in retrospect. Yet this "common-sense" meaning (as it might be termed) is at the same time meso-cosmic (to use a physical concept significant in this respect too); in other words, the inaccuracies have so negligible an effect that they can be ignored. But the inaccuracies have different consequences under macro-cosmic conditions (in this instance, totality), and need to be removed if even the common-sense application of the notion of meaning is to hold out against every consequence.

These are additional implications of the concept of progress that follow on the notion of *meaning* implied in that concept. As a particular as well as collective designation of every meaning, the *humanum* has a wide range, and cannot be restricted to anthropology pure and simple. Accordingly, with regard to the category of progress—and here precisely—there can be no new Marxist anthropology without a new Marxist cosmology.

In the history of revolution, deep faith in man and deep faith in the world have long gone hand in hand, unmoved by mechanistics and opposition to purpose. But militant optimism, as the subjective side of real progress, also implies searching for the where-to and what-for on the objective side—of forward-moving being without which there is no progressive consciousness. And the *humanum* is so *inclusive* in the *real possibility* of the *content of its goal, that it allows all movements and forms of human culture location in the togetherness of different epochs. The humanum is so strong that it does not collapse in face of a wholly mechanistically conceived cyclic time.*

Closer to us, however, a far-distant omega (this time as a goal-point that is not oriented only to the West) has to prove itself in the face of non-European history: which means in face of the non-historic but actual new start of Africa and Asia. For these continents the past of the white races is only negligibly their own too; for those nations who in various ways have enjoyed no future, history as a whole is something that begins tomorrow. The firmer the refusal of a purely Western emphasis, and of one laid solely upon development to date (to say nothing of discredited imperialism), all the stronger is the help afforded by a utopian, open and in itself still experimental orientation. Only thus can hundreds of cultures flow into the unity of the human race; a unity that only then takes shape, in non-linear historical time, and with an historical direction that is not fixed and monodic.

For the very sake of the human race, Africa and Asia join in the polyphonic chorus of a polyrhythmic advance of progress towards this unity—admittedly beneath a sun which first arose, actively and in theory, in Europe, yet one which would shine upon a community that is really without slavery. In all its revolutions, the Western concept of progress has never implied a European (and of course not an Asiatic or African) vanguard, but a better Earth for all men.

THESES

1. Progress is one of our most important and cherished concepts.

2. Any consideration and analysis of the concept of progress must bear on its social function—its why and its wherefore; for progress is a notion that can be misused and abused for the ends of a colonialist ideology.

3. The concept of progress can be applied validly to the forces of production and the economic basis; it can be relatively invalid in the case of the superstructure—or at least only faintly valid in comparison; and vice versa. The same is true of superstructures which succeed one another chronologically (cultures, civilizations): especially in the case of the category of progress in art.

4. The concept of progress will not tolerate any "cultural spheres" which require a reactionary nailing down of time to space. It requires not unilinearity but a broad, flexible and thoroughly dynamic "multiverse": the voices of history joined in perpetual and often intricate counterpoint. A unilinear model must be found obsolete if justice is to be done to the considerable amount of non-European material. It is no longer possible to work without curves in the series; without a new and complex time-manifold (the problem of "Riemannian time").

143

5. The objective that is the concern and requirement of true progress must be seen as so rich and deep in content that the diverse nations, societies and civilizations of the Earth (in all the stages of their economic and social development, and the dialectical laws governing these stages) have their place *in* it, and in striving *towards* it. Therefore the existing non-European cultures must be interpreted in the light of the philosophy of history, without the distortion of a predominantly European perspective, and without any reduction of their specific witness to the richness of human nature.

6. This objective has a human content that is not yet clearly defined, not yet manifest: a *concrete-utopian* human content. The diverse processes of history find their proper order in bearing on the deep relationship of the movement forward: a profundity so profound that all events of the entire world that are in the process of becoming find place and space in it. All earthly cultures and their inherited infrastructures are experiments, ventures and variously significant testimonies to the ultimate *humanum:* the content that must be processed out, the final and most important reference point of progress. Therefore these cultures do not converge in any one culture already existing in any one place—in one that might be thought to be "predominant," supremely "classical," or already "canonical" in its particular mode (itself only experimental). The unique point of convergence of past, present and future cultures is a human content that is nowhere as yet adequately manifest, but can certainly be appropriately anticipated.

7. Similarly with regard to the well-established existential question of a "meaning" of history, in relation to a "meaning" of the world. Here the unifying human content—the eschaton in the goal of progress—is least identical with the result already manifest in terms of men's actual lives and their cosmic environment. It is on the line of elongation of even the most distant projection to date of any goal of men or Nature. It lies in the remotest immanence of the actual possibility of men and Nature; an immanence that, despite its distance, is not closed to anticipation by the intelligence and science of mankind.

TRANSLATOR'S NOTES

I have tried to restrict these notes to explanations, references and literal renderings essential to Bloch's thought, yet outside the immediate framework of recall of an English-language reader.

J. C.

1. In a footnote to the Appendix to *Prolegomena to Any Future Metaphysics,* in which Kant reproves a reviewer for making him out to be a "higher Idealist": "By no means '*higher.*' Those lofty towers and metaphysically great men resembling them round which there is commonly a great deal of wind, are not for me. My place is the fruitful *bathos,* or bottom-land, of experience."

2. Karl Marx, Introduction to *A Critique of Hegel's Philosophy of Right.*

3. The sentimental yet egotistical young Werther, who eventually commits suicide because of the hopelessness of his passion for Lotte, is a type of the ardently feeling young lover.

4. The poet Tasso of Goethe's play *Torquato Tasso* is set against the successful diplomatist Antonio as a more intense kind of Werther out of harmony with the petty, practical demands of society. After reaching a point almost of egotistical mania in his suspicion of worldly motives, Tasso is apparently (though ambiguously) reconciled with his opposite at the end of the play.

5. Goethe's *Wilhelm Meister's Apprenticeship* is the foremost example of that primarily German form of biographical fiction, the *Bildungsroman* or *Erziehungsroman* (variously Englished as the "novel of character-formation," "educational novel," or "growing-

145

up novel," but described best by Roy Pascal as "the story of the formation of a character up to the moment when he ceases to be self-centred and becomes society-centred, thus beginning to shape his true self"). Werner, whose sister Wilhelm marries, is the business manager and enthusiastic bookkeeper of the troupe of players with which the idealistic Wilhelm becomes entangled.

6. "St. Jerome in his study" is a Renaissance theme (particularly in painting) symbolic of the Humanist immersed in his scholarly transmission and transformation of the literary tradition.

7. *"Der bestirnte Himmel"*—cf. Kant, *Critique of Practical Reason:* "Two things fill the mind with ever new and increasing wonder and awe, the more often and more intensely reflection is concerned with them: the starry heavens above me and the moral law in me."

8. Cf. the closing lines that Brecht wrote for the film version of his *Threepenny Opera.* The oppressors are eating the food of the poor who remain in the darkness outside:

> There are some who walk in darkness
> While others sit in the light.
> Though we can't see those in darkness
> The others are well in sight.

9. From Stefan George's *Komm in den totgesagten park und schau:*

> Come into the park that is said to be dead and look:
> The gleam of far-off smiling shores,
> The pure clouds' unhoped-for blue
> Enlighten the ponds and motley paths.

10. *Faust I,* "Walpurgis Night": *"Wie traurig steigt die unvollkommne Scheibe des roten Monds mit später Glut heran."* Faust and Mephistopheles are walking in the Harz Mountains; Mephisto counters Faust's description of the inspiring power of natural scenery with a caustic and wintry comment.

11. Karl Marx, Preface to the *Critique of Political Economy.*

12. From Faust's soliloquy (Part I, "Night") before the bells of Easter sound. Faust turns from looking at the skull that once sought the light of truth but strayed, to address his instruments:

146

You instruments, you mock me, not reveal,
With cylinder and cog, with cam and wheel.
I at the door and you the key (I thought);
But they'll not raise the bolt—your wards so
                                    finely wrought.
Nature is inscrutable in open day,
And will not let her veil be torn away;
What to your spirit she will not reveal,
You cannot wrest from her with levers and with
                                    steel.

13. Alcibiades' speech in Plato's *Symposium.*
14. Schiller's poem *Der Spaziergang* is too long to quote in full. The poet escapes from his room into the balm of the countryside, ascends a winding path into the dark wood and emerges to look up at the heights still before him and the valley below. He meditates on man's lot down there, and is carried back into antiquity. He reviews the growth and tribulations of mankind and then awakens from his vision of storm and stress to the consolations of enduring Nature. The poem ends with the well-known line: *"Und die Sonne Homers, siehe! sie lächelt auch uns"* ("For look, Homer's sun smiles on us too").
15. *Faust I,* "Prelude in the Theatre." The *Bretterhaus* or wooden house to which the Director refers is both the playhouse set up by the itinerant company and, eventually, the "first wooden shed" (referred to by Mephistopheles in *Faust II*) which marks the start of Faust's great constructional scheme.
16. A reference to four lines of the speech of the *Chorus Mysticus* at the end of *Faust II: "Alles Vergängliche/ Ist nur ein Gleichnis;/ Das Unzulängliche,/ Hier wird's Ereignis"* ("Everything transient is but a parable; here the inadequate is fulfilled [i.e. becomes actual]").
17. I.e. "hylics," those who have no light and cannot be saved; "psychics," those who can be saved if they keep the precepts of the Church; "pneumatics," those who have the light and can be saved.
18. *Economic and Philosophic Manuscripts of 1844,* trans. Martin Milligan, New York, 1964, p. 177.
19. *Sturm und Drang:* The main *"Stürmer und Dränger,"* as the leading figures of the German Romantic literary reaction against the

Enlightenment were known, were Schiller, Herder and the young Goethe.

20. The "*deutsche Misere*," i.e. German apathy or abjectness—a phrase of Heine's used by Marx and Engels.

21. I.e. as Mephistopheles identifies himself when interrogated by Faust in Part I.

22. In the Study scene in Part I: "Thus against the creative, healing, ever-active power/ you clench in vain your cold, malicious devil's fist."

23. At the end of Part II the angels bear aloft "*Faustens Unsterbliches*"—the immortal part of Faust—and repeat: "Him can we save whose striving never ceases."

24. In the last scene of Act V of Part II holy anchorites are in their rocky cells on the celestial mountainside. Doctor Marianus (possibly a realization of Faust), "enraptured" in the highest, purest cell, addresses the Queen of heaven:

> Highest Queen of the world,
> Let me see your mystery
> In the blue, outspreading canopy of heaven.

25. The important final passage of the *Phenomenology* reads thus: "The path leading to the goal (which is absolute knowledge, i.e. Spirit [mind] which knows itself as Spirit) is the [interiorizing] memory of historic spirits as they exist in themselves and achieve the organization of their kingdom. They are preserved in the aspect of their autonomous empirical existence (which appears in the form of contingency) as recorded *history;* but they are preserved in the aspect of their organization understood conceptually, as the *phenomenology* or science of knowledge appearing. These two, history and phenomenology, taken together as history understood conceptually, comprise the [interiorizing] memory and the calvary of Absolute Spirit, the objective reality, truth and certitude of its throne, without which it would be a solitary entity deprived of life.—From the cup of this kingdom of spirits its eternity foams up to it."

Hegel made a significant change in his closing quotation from Schiller's poem *Friendship*, the last couplet of which reads: "From the cup of the *whole* kingdom of *souls*/ Eternity foams up to him"—"him" being the Deity who achieves eternity through creation.

148

Compare another, relevant use of the figure in *The Sorrows of Werther*, Book I, Letter of August 18th: ". . . how often I have longed to fly with the wings of a crane overhead, to the shore of the unmeasured ocean; to drink that swelling joy of life from the foaming cup of the eternal; and feel, if only for a moment in the restricted power of my bosom, a single drop of the sublimity of the Being that produces everything in itself and through itself."

26. Minerva-Athene, the protectress of heroes (e.g. of Hercules and Odysseus) and patron of useful industry. There is a well-known reference of Hegel's to philosophy as the "owl of Minerva which takes wing only as twilight falls."

27. This and the subsequent quotation from Engels are taken from his *Anti-Dühring*.

28. The first volume of Friedrich Hölderlin's novel *Hyperion* was published in 1797. Hyperion, a patriotic and idealistic young Greek, disappointed at finding the anti-Turkish rebel army he joins no more than a bandit horde, and by the death of his lover Diotima, eventually arrives in Germany, but castigates the Germans for their insensibility to the beauty of Naure and to humane ideals, and returns to Greece.

29. Cf. the closing words of Marx's Introduction to *A Contribution to the Critique of Hegelian Philosophy:* "When all the conditions for the victory of the working classes are ripe, the Gallic cock will crow to announce that the day of . . . Resurrection has dawned."

30. I.e. the Introduction (1857), *not* the Preface (1859). Marx never published this less dogmatic and fragmentary Introduction, in which the remarks on the unequal relation of the material basis (Greek economy) to the cultural superstructure (Greek art) appear.

31. A superficial Danish "classical" sculptor of the nineteenth century.

32. The original is from Virgil's *Aeneid* I, 33: "*Tantae molis erat Romanan condere gentem*" ("Such toil was required to establish the Roman people"). Hegel's adaptation was preceded by Herder's motto to his *History of Humankind* (1791): ". . . *Germanas condere gentes*" (". . . to establish the German nation").

33. Some exegetes allow this interpretation of the pronouncement (Exodus 13:14), of which the usual rendering is "I AM WHO I AM." Bloch's version is also an alternative RSV rendering.

34. See n. 14 above.

149